Leipzig Mission and Dalit Christians in Pandur, Tamil Nadu

Christian Heritage Rediscovered

The Series, as the name suggests, is meant to focus on Christian Faith & Living vis-à-vis topics like Literature & Poetry, Indigenous Philosophizing, Ethical response towards Agriculture, Health & Healing, Science & Technology, Eco-feminist Theology, Sociological approach towards Human Rights, Law & Politics, Arts, History of Ideas, Ancient Civilizations, Cultural Contiguity, Religious Cosmologies & Mysticism, Footsteps of famous Theologians, World Peace & Harmony, Global Capitalism, Network Marketing, Cybertheology, Population & Demographics, Epigraphic Studies, Contextualized Education, and many others. We welcome a Mss. on any topic/s mentioned, whether they are original works, scholarly monographs, collections of conference papers, revised dissertations, or translations of historical documents. Through the Series we, the Publishers, are striving to put forward published works that may help Institutions, Academic Bodies, Researchers, Scholars and the World at large in furthering their respective knowledge and understanding on the concerned subject. We welcome your comments on our efforts and further suggestions on how we can foster the upcoming thought provoking theologically grounded books.

Christian Heritage Rediscovered - 52

Leipzig Mission and Dalit Christians in Pandur, Tamil Nadu

Jayabalan Murthy

CWI

Christian World Imprints™

First Published in 2017 by

Christian World Imprints(TM)
Christian Publishing & Books from India
H-12 Bali Nagar, **New Delhi-110015**
info@christianworldimprints.com
www.ChristianWorldImprints.com
Phone: +91 11 25465925

ISBN: 978-93-5148-190-4 (HB)   ISBN: 978-93-5148-191-1 (PB)

Cataloging in Publication Data--DK
Courtesy: D.K. Agencies (P) Ltd. <docinfo@dkagencies.com>

Murthy, Jayabalan, 1982- author.
Leipzig mission and dalit Christians in Pandur, Tamil Nadu / Jayabalan Murthy.
pages cm. -- (Christian heritage rediscovered ; 52)
ISBN 9789351481904 (HB)
ISBN 9789351481911 (PB)

1. Leipziger Mission (Germany : East). 2. Missions--India--Pāndūr. 3. Church work with people with social disabilities--India--Pāndūr. 4. Dalits--India--Pāndūr. 5. Christians--India--Pāndūr. I. Title. II. Series: Christian heritage rediscovered ; 52.

BV3265.3.M87 2017   DDC 266.415482 23

Photo Courtesy Details: Siebenundachhtzigster Jahresbericht: *der Evanglisch Lutherischen mission zu Leipzig vom 1 januar bis 31 Dezember 1905,* (Leipzig: Drud von Böschel & Trepte. 1906)

Printed in India.

I like to Dedicate this book to the First
missionary our Lord and saviour Jesus christ
and Missionaries, Pastors, Catechist and Bible
women who worked in Pandur Tamilnadu for the
empowerment of Pandur Dalits.

Contents

Forewords xi
Acknowledgement xvii
Abbreviations xix

Chapter 1: Introduction 1
1.1. Dalits in India 1
1.2. Dalit Christians 3
1.3. Hypothesis and Research questions 4
1.4. Methods 6
1.5. Informants 6

Chapter 2: Background of Pandur 7
2.1. The Tamil people and caste system 7
2.2. Fifth Caste 8
2.3. Brahminic culture 9
2.4. Names given by other 9
2.5. The Term "Dalit" 10
2.6. Etymology 10
2.7. Tamil Nadu under Colonialism 11
2.8. Background of Thiruvallur district 12
2.9. Geographical 12
2.10. Pandur 13
2.11. Pandur pastorate 13

2.12. Social, Economical, Educational and Religious background of in and around Pandur 13
2.12.1. Social status 14
2.12.2. Dwelling place of Dalit 15
2.12.3. Economic 16
2.12.4. Education 17
2.12.5. Religious background 17
2.12.6. Mass Conversion 18
2.12.7. The background of early Christians in and around Pandur 19

Chapter 3: Arrival and Mission Methods of Leipzig Evangelical Lutheran Missionaries 21
3.1. Protestant Mission in India 21
3.1.1. Arrival of Bartholomew Ziegenbalg and Henry Plütschau 22
3.1.2. Dark period of Halle Mission 23
3.2. Anglican Period 24
3.3. Leipzig Evangelical Lutheran Mission 25
3.3.1. History of Leipzig Mission 25
3.3.2. Leipzig Mission in India 26
3.4. Leipzig Missionaries in Pandur 27
3.4.1. Rev. Johannes Kabis 27
3.4.2. Rev. Rudolf Enno Schomerus 27
3.4.3. Rev. Elias Soederstroem 28
3.4.4. Rev. Karl Heller 28
3.4.5. Rev. Wilhelm Ruckdaeschel 28
3.4.6. Rev. Karl Kannegiesser 29
3.4.7. Miss Elisabeth Buchholz 29
3.4.8. Sister Johanna Zimmermann 29
3.4.9. Rev. Hans Woxblom 30
3.4.10. Miss Marie Haback 30
3.4.11. Luise Fröhlich 30
3.4.12. Silesia Lüben Ruhnke Lydia 31

3.5. Mission Methods of Leipzig Mission Societies 31
3.5.1. Education 32
3.5.2. Sewing school 33
3.5.3. Girls Hostel 34
3.5.4. Heller Boys Hostel 34
3.5.5. Kindergarten 34
3.5.6. Medical work 35
3.5.7. Distributions of land 35
3.5.8. Voice for the voice less 36
3.5.9. Agricultural school 37
3.5.10. Cemetery 37
3.5.11. Well 38
3.6. Evangelistic Work 39
3.6.1. Church planting 40
3.6.2. Catechumens 41
3.7. Intervention of war 41
3.8. Swedish Mission in India 42
3.9. Tamil Evangelical Lutheran Church 43

Chapter 4: Evaluating the Motives and Methods of Leipzig Mission through the voices of Pandur Dalit Christians 45
4.1. Inducement 45
4.1.1. Imperialism 46
4.1.2. Driving Force 47
4.1.3. Sacred and Secular 48
4.2. Education and accommodation 48
4.2.1. Exposure 50
4.2.2. Breaking the barriers 50
4.2.3. Healing 51
4.2.4. Income 52
4.2.5. Female empowerment 54
4.2.6. Undignified to Dignified 55

4.2.7. Forerunners for counter culture 56
4.2.8. Purpose of Religion 56
4.3. Living with the people 57
4.3.1. Identified with the Dalits 57
4.3.2. House Visiting 57
4.3.3. Bible women 58
4.3.4. Accepting the local Culture 59
4.4. Living Christian values 59
4.4.1. Caring and sharing 59
4.4.2. Prayerful and Faithful Life 60
4.4.3. Missionary accountability 60
4.5. Challenges 61
4.5.1. Famine 61
4.5.2. Casteism 61
4.6. Present LELM Projects in Pandur 62
4.6.1. Mission to the North 63
4.6.2. Volunteers program 63
4.6.3. Supporting the Dalit children 63

Chapter 5: Conclusion **65**

Bibliography 69

Appendix A: List of Interviewees 73
Appendix B: Questionnaire 75
Appendix C: Maps and Photos 77

Foreword-I

The Leipzig mission has long been the largest Lutheran Mission in Germany as well as the Hermannsburg mission in India. Both are committed mission organizations of the German Lutherans in India. In Germany, the two missionary societies fought over their attitude towards the caste issue in India. Historically, the Hermannsburg mission is against the caste system, since it is contrary to the message of the New Testament. The Lepziger mission is regarded as more open in matter. It is the merit of the master's thesis, which was written in the program founded by me Intercultural Theology at the Georg-August University of Göttingen to have corrected the image with respect to the Leipzig missionaries and their work in India. Jayabalan Murthy was able to show that the Leipzig mission is overcoming the caste issues by preaching and social work. This has contributed to and has called for the liberation of the Dalits in India on the basis of the example of the Christians in Pandur. The Faculty of theology in Göttingen is one of the faculties in Germany, which has a long tradition in the study of India and of Christianity in India. Jayabalan Murthy's book shows that student contributions and important observations can contribute alot to this matter and help him further deepen the present study as a scientific contribution in the form of a dissertation. For this reason, he has been working for some time now as a Ph.d. student with me. His investigations to the Leipzig mission represent important steps for the development of the German and Swedish archive material for the Indian church history. The present single study into Pandur shows the contribution of the German Lutheran mission to the emancipation of Dalits from Indian perspective in Tamil Nadu.

Prof. Dr. Dr. h. c. mult. Martin Tamcke
Faculty of Theology
Georg-August-Universität Göttingen, Germany

Foreword-II

The place Pandur in Tamil Nadu is well known in the Leipzig Mission History.

Since the time of missionary Johannes Kabis until now the relationship to the Christian community never broke. With Mr. Jayabalan Murthy´s present work we have now a very detailed and well readable book about this special mission area. The author does not only describe historical facts but also the motives and methods of Leipzig Mission. He does not end with programmes and projects in the past. He also brings very new activities of the Leipzig Mission – like the "volunteer-programme" and the "Mission to the North Programme" – to their necessarily attention. Leipzig Mission is very grateful for this research on mission history and today's partnership. We wish the book serves a lot of readers out of all generations to be a motivation to further engagement.

Rev. Ravinder Salooja
Leipzig Mission Work Director
Germany

Rev. Hans-Georg Tannhäuser
Secretary for Asia/ Pacific Leipzig Mission
Germany

Foreword-III

Since the beginning of the British colonial government, it was customary to describe India as a caste-ridden society, in which the values of the so-called caste-Hindus determine the lifestyle. A view, commonly held among the so-called 'Orientalists', was that the Hindus were linked to a rigid, hierarchical and Brahmin–dominated value system, in which individualism did not play any role, and from where there was no way of escape for the individual. In recent times, this view has been cast into doubt. The European view of the caste system, as it has been argued, played a crucial role in defining the Indian society as traditional and consolidating the caste system, which the Europeans endorsed and thus constituting the Indian social structure.

This book shows that this common view has to be put into question. The German missionaries, who worked in Tamil Nadu in the 19th century, comprehended the Indian Society as reflected in their own parishes. The majority of the Christians in Tamil Nadu were Dalits and members of various ethnic Śūdra groups. The need to acquire a thorough knowledge of the structure of Indian society arose out of the practical missionary work and its subsequent theological considerations. The question concerning the relationship between the small Christian minority and the Indian society at large also determined the concept with which the missionaries carried out their mission work. Their approach to the principles of comprehension and classification was inevitably euro-centric. The prominent issue for the missionaries, whether the caste differences and local rituals were compatible with the Christian faith, depended on the individual assessment and theological conviction, and had its impact on the understanding of the Indian social system.

Jayabalan Murthy's study of the Dalit Christians in Pandur in Tamil Nadu focuses on the caste images of the Leipzig missionaries and convincingly he shows of what eminent importance the contribution of the Dalits has been to the building of a Lutheran Church. His analysis of the conceptions of caste at the time of the Leipzig missionaries does not only rely on western documents like mission reports and letters of the missionaries, but the importance of this research work is that it shed light on the perspective of the Christian Dalits themselves, by listening to their voices and by searching for hidden transcripts of their voices in the archives.

The method with which the German Lutheran missionaries treated the caste problem indicated nevertheless, that hegemonic claims existed in the thinking of Graul, Ochs and others as well. The moral superiority of the Christianized West is frequently emphasized in their accounts. They left no doubt about the fact that the Indian society was in need of a 'moral' revival. The question had to be raised whether this revival should have taken place with reference to an ethos, which the missionaries identified as traditionally Indian, or whether this revival also entailed the adoption of a Western lifestyle. In this they distinguished themselves from their British missionary colleques.

Because of their long years of service in India and their extensive knowledge of the local conditions, as well as their critical distance to the East India Company, many missionaries took an independent position from the official discourse with the Orientalistic researches when observing and reflecting on the Indian society. Jayabalan Murthy offers a detailed account of one of the prominent parishes and villages in which the Leipzig mission was active and thus opens the reader's eyes to a complex intercultural exchange project that resulted in an independent Tamil Church.

Prof. Dr. Andreas Nehring
Friedrich-Alexander-Universität Erlangen-Nürnberg
Germany

Acknowledgement

I thank God from the bottom of my heart for enabling me to carry out this research. Also, I want to thank the Georg-August Universität Göttingen for granting me permission to publish my Masters of Intercultural Theology thesis. The present form is revised with a change in title and also certain additions and corrections in content. Therefore, I am responsible for the revised format of this work and its changed title.

I solemnly thank my thesis supervisors Prof. Dr. Wilhelm Richebächer and Prof. Dr. Martin Tamcke who have been the motivator of my efforts and made helpful suggestions from time to time to complete my thesis.

I wish to extend my heartfelt gratitude towards George -August-Universität Göttingen University and Fachhochsule für interkulturelle Theologie Hermannsburg for molding me in my theological journey. I thank the authorities and Library staff who have helped me in one way or the other. I like to thank Evangelical Lutheran Mission who supported financially for my studies.

My sincere thanks also go to, Leipzig Evangelical Lutheran mission and Pandur Dalit Christians for providing me the opportunity for interviews. I thank my friends who helped me to spend their time to discuss and suggesting corrections in this work.

The purpose of this acknowledgement would indeed look incomplete without expressing my deepest thanks to my parents, wife and my little daughter keziha Jessica who supported me through their prayers, love and encouragement.

Abbreviations

B. C.	-	Backward Class
CSM	-	Church of Swedish Mission
KM	-	Kilo Meters
N.D.	-	No Date
LELM	-	Leipzig Evangelical Lutheran Mission
SPG	-	Society for the Propagation of the Gospel
SPCK	-	Society for Promoting Christian Knowledge
T.E.L.C	-	Tamil Evangelical Lutheran Church
Vol.	-	Volume

Chapter 1

Introduction

1.1. Dalits in India

India's caste system gives individuals a certain hierarchical status according to Hindu beliefs. Traditionally, there are four major castes (divided into many sub-categories) and one group of people fall outside the caste system and they are called Dalits. As members of the lowest category in the Indian society, Dalits face discrimination at almost every level of their day to day life: from access to education and medical amenities to restrictions as to where they can live and what jobs they can have. The discrimination against Dalits is a serious matter because the number of Dalits affected is approximately 167 million in India, constituting over 16 percent of the total population.[1]

Dalits are divided into leather- workers, street sweepers, cobblers, agricultural bonded laborers and manual scavengers. The latter group is considered the lowest of the low and they are officially estimated at one million. Traditionally, they are the ones who are responsible for digging village graves, disposing of dead bodies of animals and playing drums at funerals. Approximately three-quarters of the Dalit

1 http://navsarjan.org/navsarjan/Dalits/whoareDalits accessed on 24.5.2015.

workforce are in the agricultural sector of the economy. The country's population is 1.28 billion and in this 40 million people is Dalits and they are bonded laborers. These jobs rarely provide sufficient income to feed their families or to send their children to school. As a result, many Dalits are impoverished, uneducated and illiterate. Dalits have been oppressed, culturally subjugated, and politically marginalized. The principles of untouchiblity, purity and pollution dictate what Dalits are, what they are not allowed to do, where they are not allowed to live, go or sit, who they can and cannot give water, and whom to eat with or marry extending into the minutiae of all aspects of daily life.[2]

According to the 2011 census Dalits, officially known as schedule castes, constitute 201 million people. This figure does not include Dalits who have converted or are born and raised within a non-Hindu religious community. It is therefore more than likely that the total number of Dalit population- including the millions of Dalit Muslims and Christians- far exceeds the official figure of 201 million.[3]

The number of Hindu Dalits is approximately over 160 million, and together with Muslim, Buddhist, and Christian 'untouchables' the number adds up to a phenomenal 240 million approximately and that means almost one quarter of the Indian population. Up until the present day they are often extremely discriminated against by caste Indians, and in some cases they are also the ones experiencing persecution and violence. They are to some extent outside of the caste system or on its lowest rung, and for that reason considered to be unclean, untouchable and unseeable, particularly in rural areas. This discrimination is up until the present day a reality in most parts of India, something that in the West is often viewed as a form of racism or slavery. This can go so far as to mean that contact with their shadows must be avoided because even a low cast person's shadow can pollute. Again and again they are the victims of violence

2 http://navsarjan.org/navsarjan/Dalits/whoareDalits accessed on 24.5.2015.

3 http://idsn.org/countries/india/ accessed on 24.5.2015.

and land confiscation." Even to today 400,000 to perhaps 800,000 Dalits clean latrines daily with their bare hands.[4]

1.2. Dalit Christians

In 1950, the Indian constitution abolished untouchiblity, classifying the untouchables as scheduled castes and tribes; in doing so it also provided a system of affirmative action (called the reservation policy) whereby 22.5 percent of all government and semi government jobs including seats in Parliament and state legislatures was reserved for those castes; the law also provided space for admission to schools and colleges with the rider that Reservation Privilege is applicable only for those Dalits who follow *Hinduism*, or *Buddhism,* or *Sikhism*. According to the constitution and legal code Dalits who convert to Christianity and Islam lose their legal status as Dalits and with that the financial and legal support to which they are entitled. Using the logic that as Muslims or Christians they no longer belong to the lowest order of society, they lose their constitutional rights, i.e., they are no more Schedule Caste *Adi dravidars*; they are classified as B.C. (Backward Class).[5]

In 1980, the constitutional policy was extended to cover the rest of the 3,743 backward castes in the country. But, Christians who claim 'no caste' are not included in the quotas, meaning those Dalits who convert to Christianity are no longer part of the affirmative action program run by the government. Dalit Christians have now appealed to the government to extend the benefits of reservation policy to Dalit Christians in order to improve their employment opportunities. In 2008, a study commissioned by the National commission for minorities suggested extension of reservation to Dalit Muslims and Dalit Christians. According to the study, Indian Muslims and Christians should be brought under the ambit of the constitutional safeguards.[6]

---

4 http://www.thomasschirrmacher.net/blog/when-indian Dalits-convert-to-christianity-or-islam-they-lose-social-welfare-benefits-and-rights-they-are-guaranteed-under-the-constitution/ accessed on 24.5.2015.

5 http://www.rediff.com/news/2005/feb/11Dalit.htm accessed on 24.5.2015.

6 Ibid.

When missionaries came to India to proclaim the Gospel, majority of the people who embraced Christianity were Dalits. When missionaries saw that the Dalits were discriminated by Hindu High caste people they tried their best to liberate them and help them to come out of all sorts of discriminations in their life and attain a good level in society. Even though, Government refuses to accept Dalit Christians under the reservation policy and give them welfare, the Christian institutions, i.e., colleges and schools etc. give first preference to the Dalit Christians. But it cannot be compensated for the welfare which the Hindu Dalits get from the Government. Being a Dalit Christian in India is not an easy task. A Dalit Christian must forgo lots of privileges.

In my research I am going to expose the discriminations suffered by the Pandur Dalits and how the Leipzig Evangelical Missionaries helped them to overcome their situations. The Leipzig Evangelical Lutheran Mission (LELM) was a major mission in Pandur near Chennai. Pandur is intimately associated with Rev. Johannes Kabis who came to India in 1877. Pandur has been a thriving Christian centre for decades with a strong Christian congregation, Church and several institutions. These Christians are descendants of Dalits (former untouchable Paraiyars) who embraced Christianity. From a life of near slavery, poverty, illiteracy, oppression and indignity, conversion to Christianity transformed the lives of these people. In this study I propose to elucidate the role of Leipzig missionaries in the social, economic, educational and spiritual life of Pandur Dalits.

1.3. Hypothesis and Research questions

Pandur Dalits found liberation and have made significant progress only because of Christian missionaries of Leipzig Mission. It raises two important questions: 1).What do the Dalit Christians of Pandur feel about the role of Leipzig missionaries in the liberation of their ancestors from various forms of oppression? 2).What progress have they made in their social, economic, educational and spiritual life since their conversion?

To answer these questions some other questions must be answered first and they are as follows:

1. What was the background of Pandur and Dalit Christians?

The first chapter answers this question. It will focus on the Social, Religious, Education and Economic background of the people who are living in and around Pandur. It gives a geographical background of Thiruvallur and Pandur. An attempt is made to give a clear-cut understanding about Casteism in the Indian society and the pathos of the Dalit people who lived in and around Pandur, where the Leipzig and Swedish missionaries had worked. The missionary's work of conversion into Christianity has made a great impact on the social and secular status of people in and around Pandur. Most of the converts once belonged to the depressed community in this area. They were considered as the so-called lower caste and outcaste or untouchables. Their Conversion into Christianity offered them an opportunity to break the chains of slavery to the casteist Hinduism. The new religion offered them self-respect, education, value and dignity.

2. What are the mission methods Leipzig Evangelical missions used to liberate the Dalits in and around Pandur?

This question is answered in chapter two. This chapter is a brief sketch on the beginning of the Protestant Missions in India with special reference to areas in and around Pandur. This chapter highlights the methods used by the Leipzig Evangelical Lutheran Mission (LELM), in dealing with the Pandur Dalits and the resulting changes including the cultural identity of the local people. It is an account of how the depressed communities were restored their selfhood through conversion into the Christian faith.

3. What do the Dalit Christians of Pandur feel about the role of Leipzig missionaries and about their methods in the liberation of their ancestors from various forms of oppression?

In chapter four, this question will be answered. What motivated the Leipzig Missionaries to launch the kind of social work they did? Was religious conversion the only motive? This is a common question in many. Let us also evaluate the motive of the mission methods used by the missionaries. What are the challenges LELM faced in their field and what is the present project they are involved in Pandur.

1.4. Methods

Of course, the answers to the questions raised above do not come from me but from the Dalit Christians themselves who are the beneficiaries of the mission's work. Interviews were conducted across a broad spectrum of Dalit Christians in and around Pandur, and also among the descendents of the missionaries who dedicated their life and work to this work. All the interviews are recorded on mobile phone and are available for anyone to listen. The research is a descriptive study which also includes both library and empirical studies.

1.5. Informants

The key informants for this research are the archival materials of the then Leipzig Mission Society and Halle, Dalits in around Pandur, selected Dalit Christian Families converted by Leipzig Missionaries, and the knowledgeable pastors, teachers, students and employees connected with the Pandur Church and institutions such as Kabis Higher Secondary School, Children's Home, Boys' Hostel, Girls' Hostel, Tailoring School and Dispensary, articles, books, journals and online materials.

Chapter 2

Background of Pandur

Introduction

This chapter will focus Social, Religious, Educational and Economic background of the people who are living in and around of Pandur, it gives Geographical background of Thiruvallur and Pandur. And attempt is made to give clear cut understanding about Casteism in Indian society and pathos of the Dalit people who lived in and around Pandur, where the Leipzig and Swedish missionaries had worked. The missionary's work of conversion into Christianity has made a great impact on the social and secular status of in and around Pandur. Most converts belonged to the depressed community in this area. They were considered to be the so-called lower caste and outcaste or untouchables. Their Conversion into Christianity offered them an opportunity to break the chains of slavery from a casteist Hinduism. The new religion offered them Self-respect, education, value and dignity.

2.1. The Tamil people and caste system

The population in Thiruvallur and Pandur are Tamil people. Traditionally, sociological identity was found by the population of Tamilnadu in a particular *jati* or strictly endogamous caste group to which one belonged by birth for one's life. Apart from certain tribes, who were settled in the hills. Or other remote places, or moving about as migrants, society was composed of diverse local units, in which various *jati* formed and reformed a hierarchal but mobile system of interdependency within and outside the *vedic* frame work of the *avarnas: Brahmans,*[7] *Kshatriyas,*[8] *Vaisyas,*[9] and *sudras,*[10] of which the first and the fourth only were originally held to be really represented in Tamilnadu.[11]

2.2. Fifth Caste

There is one more group of people placed still lower and outside the caste-system altogether were 'outcastes' or exterior castes'- latter called Panchamas (fifth caste), Depressed Classes, Harijans or Adidravidars and Paraiyars. The Paraiyars, the largest group among them, from whom the term 'Pariah' was derived for the whole category, were field laborers and village servants with the obligation to function as drummers (parai) at Hindu ceremonies[12] and to announce events to people, usually with the drum called parai. From parai comes the caste name *Paraiyan* and its European derivative, Pariah[13] were most

7 The *Brahmins*, the priestly class came from the head of God. They are eligible for learning and teaching and perform sacrifices. The others cannot teach and perform sacrifice.

8 The *Kshatriyas*, the warrior class came from the shoulder of God. They are eligible for learning. Their work is to protect the people by waging war against the enemies.

9 The *Vaysias,* the trading class came from the thigh of God. Their work is to trade and feed the above two classes.

10 The *Sudras,* the servants came from the feet of God and their work is to do all menial works to the above three Classes. They are not entitled to learn anything.

11 Hugald Grafe, *History of Christianity in Tamilnadu from 1800 to 1975*, (Bangalore: Church History Association of India, 1990), 14.

12 S. Manickam, *The Social Setting of Christian Conversion in South India: The Impact of the Wesleyan Methodist Missionaries on the Tiruchi-Tanjore-Diocese with Special Reference to the Harijan Communities of the Mass Movement Area, 1820-1937* (Wiesbaden: Franz Steiner Verlag, 1977), 28.

13 Dennis Hudson, Protestant Origins in India: Tamil Evangelical Christians, 1706-1835 (Richmond: William B. Eerdmans Publishing Company, 2000), 76.

numerous in Chengalpattu District the below them, finally, ranged the Pallars (servants), the Chakkiliyars or Madharis (their proper Tamil name), who were cobblers and agricultural laborers with their largest number in Coimbatore[14] and the Tottis (sweepers).

2.3. Brahminic culture

The Hindu caste structure, throughout the past 3000 year of its survival, has been victorious in construct a culture, an oppressive Brahminic culture and has succeeded in making the Dalits personalize its values. The following are some of its features which have direct attitude on the Dalits to construct their oppression complete. The caste structure and the oppressive culture it culture it trick to create have succeeded in canonizing the Brahmin as Law giver and norm setter while accusing the Dalit as followers without any right for self-determination. Because of the Brahmin's patronage to God, Brahmin has come to be seen as God. The universe is under the power of gods; the gods are the power of the mantras; the mantras under the Brahmins; therefore Brahmins are our gods. Dalits, who traditionally did not have a hereditary priesthood Dalit theologian Dr. Devasahayam says Dalits are true Lutherans who believed in the priesthood of all believers- have of late stated inviting Brahmin priests for their religious ceremonies. This Brahminic culture has created a sense of inferiority complex psychologically it created in the Dalits a lowered self esteem and confusion of self-identity.[15]

2.4. Names given by other

In earlier days Dalits are known by many other names, which were/are given to them by others, mainly to despise them or to show contempt. These include: *Dasa, Dasysu, Raksasa, Asura, Avarna, Nisada, Panchama (5th Caste), Mletcha, Svapaca, Chandala (Gupta Rule), Achchuta, Harijan (Gandhi)*, Exterior Castes, Depressed Classes (British rule), Scheduled Castes (Indian Constitution),

14 S. Manickam, *The Social Setting of Christian Conversion in South India,* 28.

15 V. Devasahayam, *Outside the Camp: Bible Studies in Dalit Perspective* (Madras: Gurukul Lutheran Theological College & Research Institute, 1992), 28.

Untouchables, etc.[16] Besides these names, there are a number of other titles or names which have been given to them at the regional language level. For example, *Chura* in Punjab (North West India); *Bhangi* or *Lal-Beghi* in Hindi (North India); *Mahar* in Marathi (Central India); *Mala* in Telugu, *Paraiyan* in Tamil, and *Pulayan* in Malayalam (South India).[17] All this names are given by other.

2.5. The Term "Dalit"

These names given by others to Dalits carry within them the virus of a binary opposition of the "we-the-pure" and "you-the-impure." In reaction to these names which attribute hereditary impurity to "untouchables," the "untouchables" choose to give a name to them and the name is Dalit.[18] Mahatma Jotiba Phule (1826-1890), used it to describe the outcasts and untouchables as the oppressed and broken victims of Indian caste-ridden society.[19] However, it is Dr. B. R. Ambedkar (1891-1956) who brought it to the limelight.[20] But it was only in 1970s, that the followers of the Dalit Panther Movement of Maharashtra gave currency to the term "Dalit" as a constant reminder of their age-old subjugation, denoting both their state of deprivation and the people who are oppressed.[21]

2.6. Etymology

The word "Dalit," in Sanskrit is both used as noun and an adjective. As a noun, Dalit can be used for all three genders, masculine,

16 V. Devasahayam, "Pollution, Poverty and Powerlessness," in Arvind P. Nirmal (ed) *A Reader in Dalit Theology* (Chennai: Gurukul Lutheran Theological College & Research Institute, 2007), 1.

17 James Massey, *Roots: A Concise History of Dalits* (Delhi: The Indian Society for Promoting Christian Knowledge, 1994, 1991), 7.

18 Antony Raj "The Dalit Christian Reality in Tamilnadu," *Jeevadhara* 22 (1992), 95-112, 96.

19 Eleanor Zelliot, *From Untouchable to Dalit* (New Delhi: Manohar Publication, 1992), 271.

20 James Massey, *Roots: A Concise History of Dalits,* 6.

21 See "*Dalit Panthers Manifesto,*" in Barbara R. Joshi, ed., *Untouchable, Voice of the Dalit Liberation Movement* (Delhi: Select Book Service Syndicate, 1986), pp. 141-147.

feminine and neuter. It has been derived from the root "*dal*" which means to crack, open, split, etc. "Dalit," has come to mean, things or persons burst, split, broken or torn asunder, downtrodden, scattered, crushed, destroyed, etc.[22] The term "Dalit" has also its parallel in Hebrew with the root "*dal*" means low, weak, poor, helpless, etc.[23]

According to a Dalit theologian Mr. Antony Raj the word Dalit indicates a number of things: (i) it obviously recognizes their oppressors. If today the Dalits are reduced to a life of miserable poverty and treated as impure human beings, it is the non-Dalits that must be seen as the cause of their dehumanization. (ii) The word connotes the consciousness of their own unfree existence and outcast experience, a consciousness, which forms the basis for a new cultural unity and Dalit ideology. The core of such an ideology is freedom and humanism. (iii) The term Dalit indicates is a symbol of commitment to change, confrontation and revolution.[24] At present, this term is used frequently and has become popular among the Dalits of various protest movements in India.

2.7. Tamil Nadu under Colonialism

From the beginning of the 19th century for almost one and a half centuries - with the exception of Pudukkotai, the Tamil area of the Maharaja of Travancore and a few European settlements along the coast of Pondicherry and Karaikal where only the French ruled -Tamil Nadu was ruled directly by the British Government. The Dutch territories in Tuticorin, Porto Novo, Pulicat and Sadras were permanently acquired by the British in 1825, the Danish territories in Tranquebar in 1845. The consolidated rule of the British was carried out through the Madras Presidency of the East Indian Company, a political entity much larger than the present Tamil Nadu.[25]

22 James Massey, *Roots: A Concise History of Dalit*, 6.

23 James Massey, "Christian Dalits: A Historical Perspective," *Journal of Dharma* 16 (1991), pp. 44-60, 44.

24 Antony Raj, "The Dalit Christian Reality in Tamilnadu," *Jeevadhara* 22 (1992), 95-112, 96.

25 Hugald Grafe, *History of Christianity in Tamilnadu from 1800 to 1975*, 13.

2.8. Background of Thiruvallur district

History of Thiruvallur district in Tamil Nadu is interrelated to the rule of the Pallavas, the Golkondas, the Mughals, the French, the Dutch and also the British. This district in the state of Tamil Nadu in the southern parts of India has been engraved out by the bifurcation of the previous Chengalpattu district. The towns and villages of this region became the scene of the Carnatic war. Battles were believed to be fought in this region during the struggle for supremacy between the English and French. The Pulicat town was the first Dutch possession in India founded in the year 1609 which was yield to the British East Indian Company in the year 1825. With this, the region came under the British rule which ended on the 15th of August, 1947 when India became independent.[26]

2.9. Geographical

Thiruvallur is one of the fastest growing districts of Tamil Nadu in terms of economy and human population. Geographically the district situated between 12°15', 13°15' North latitude, 79°15', and 80°20' East longitude. Geographical cover of the district is 3422 km. The district has Kancheepuram, Vellore, Bay of the Bengal and Andhra Pradesh as South, West, East, and North borders, respectively.[27]

Thiruvallur indicates the sleeping place of the holy lord 'Balaji' in the Veeraragava temple of Thiruvallur. Later, people of this area started to refer to it by names such as Trivellore and Thiruvallur. Today, this district of the Tamil Nadu state is well known, and one of the reasons behind it is the presence of the Veeraragava temple in the district. The new moon day is considered to be greatly auspicious for the lord and also for the people of this region.[28]

Missionary Alwin Gehring also mentioned about this festival in the book entitled "*Johannes Kabis Ein Vater der Paria.*"

The forming of a special administrative district capital of Madras is surrounded by the province Sengelpat, now it's called Chengalpattu

26 http://www.indianetzone.com/47/history_tiruvallur_district.htm 17.2.15.

27 http://saspublisher.com/wp-content/uploads/2014/04/SAJB-24295-306.pdf accessed on 24.2.15.

28 http://www.indianetzone.com/47/history_tiruvallur_district.htm 17.2.15.

which also includes the north western district of Triwallur location with the same name, distinguished by its huge and famous Vishnu Temple capital. Here, maintain especially on the new moon day thousands of Madraser (people who live in Madras) worshiping Hindu goddess and bathe in the great temple ponds.[29]

2.10. Pandur

Pandur is a Village in Poondi Taluk in Thiruvallur District of Tamil Nadu State, India. It is located 6 KM towards west from District head quarters Tiruvallur. (See: Appendix C Map Pandur and its surroundings) 51 KM from State capital Chennai,[30] according to population census 2011[31] the total number residing families in Pandur are 414 families. The Pandur village has population of 1979 of which 935 are males while 1044 are females.[32]

2.11. Pandur pastorate

1901 Pandur was bifurcated from Thiruvallur and made separate pastorate. Under Pandur they were 14 villages. Pattrai Perrambathur, Kaiwandur, Vedaiur, Kanachawallipuram, Nellvail, Nambakkam, Narhtavada, Ramancheri, Kawatipuram, Annaipakam, Mudur, Karani, Sendrapallyam and Placepallyam.[33]

2.12. Social, Economical, Educational and Religious background of in and around Pandur

Dalits have been the most degraded, downtrodden, exploited and the least educated in our Indian society. They have been socially and culturally, economically and politically subjugated and marginalized

---

29 Alwin, Gehring, *Johannes Kabis Ein Vater der Paria* (Leipzig: Erlagen der evanglich Lutherlichen mission, n.d.), 46. Transalted by Irene Heinke.

30 http://www.onefivenine.com/india/villages/Thiruvallur/Poondi/Pandur accessed on 2.3.15.

31 The official census in India is calculated every 5 years. The most recent one was conducted in the year 2011. The entire process was done in 2 main phases of house listing and population listing respectively.

32 http://www.census2011.co.in/city.php

33 Catharine Vimala, *Pandur in Tranquebar Mission History* (Chennai: Bethel, 2009), 26-27.

through three thousand years of our history and remain so, even after half-a-century of protective discrimination (as Scheduled Castes) under the aegis of the Government of India. Even today they are denied individual and social identity (self-respect and status). The Dalits form the inner core of poverty, which is birth-ascribed.[34] Even today the individual and social identities of Dalit denied then just imagine how it was in 19th centuries.

The Dalit were always consider as impure and polluted community by High Caste this idea of pollution may not be as old as the casts system but it is to be clearly seen in *manusmriti*: Manu rather codified and sanctioned it. *Mansusmirti* marks off this group as untouchable and unseeable, whose touch, shadow and even sight pollute the people of the other castes. Dalits should shout or ring the bell if a caste Hindu approaches them and it is also pointed out the Brahmin girl would wash her eyes if she happened to see a Dalit. Dalits were considered impure due to the fact of their birth and polluting professions, like burring the dead body, beating drums on the funeral because the drums are made by dead animal skin so its polluted and the person who touch the dead body and touch the skin of the animal are polluted according to the Hindu beliefs. Due to this and hence were banned from the temples, religious processions and schools public wells, walking through Hindu streets and also from obtaining the services of barbers and dohbies.[35]

2.12.1. Social status

As we have seen above the professions were considered to be polluting to the individual and this pollution was considered transmittable. Due to this, Dalits were banned from full participation in Indian social life. They were physically isolated from the surrounding community. For instance, Dalit could not be priest in a Hindu temple even in some parts in India Dalit could not enter into a temple. Other castes

34 M.E. Prabhakar, "The Search for a Dalit Theology," in M.E. Prabhakar, ed., *Toward a Dalit Theology* (Delhi: The Indian Society for Promoting Christians Knowledge,1988), 40.

35 V. Devasahayam, "Pollution, Poverty and Powerlessness," in Arvind P. Nirmal (ed) *A Reader in Dalit Theology*, 4.

took elaborate precautions to prevent incidental contact with Dalits. This was the same reality in Pandur.

The following voice of the Dalit who lives in Pandur can explain the social status of Dalit in Pandur.

> "If accidentally the high caste man's clothes touched by the Dalit the high caste will remove their clothes and take bath. Only then he will enter in to his house because the Dalits are untouchable and impure."[36]

Dalits are not allowed to drink from the same wells, wear shoes in the presence of an upper caste, wear full dress like an upper caste and drink from the same cups in tea stalls.[37] According to the Laws of Manu, drinking from a vessel after a Dalit used it would cause spiritual impurity of members of the higher castes. This kind social discrimination is a common practice in India. Dalits in Pandur also faced this kind of discrimination. The following two incidents can explain how the Dalits are discriminated.

> "A Dalit wearing a pant and full-hand shirt entered an upper caste village area. The upper caste people tied him to a tree and beat him severely for the crime of being born as a Dalit. A Dalit should not dress decently like upper caste people."[38]
>
> Mr. Pannerselvam said "in the 1900's in tea shops the used two cups one for Dalit and another one is for High caste."[39]

2.12.2. Dwelling place of Dalit

The Dalits as the lowest group in the caste system with stigma of untouchiblity attached to them. As more than 90% of the Dalits live in villages and huge majority depend on agriculture, they contribute

36 Mr. Samraj interviewed 18 November 2014 in Kanakaranee

37 http://news.nationalgeographic.com/news/2003/06/0602_030602_untouchables.html accessed on 24.2.15.

38 Mr. Samraj, interviewed 18 Novemeber 2014 in Kanakaranee.

39 Mr. Pannerselvam interviewed 20 November 2014 in Pandur.

excessively to the landless agriculture labors. There are many who are too poor to build their houses on their own lands, leave alone the quality of their houses. In most villages they have to suffer residential segregation.[40] Dalits keep on living in outside borders of the Hindu caste society with the labels "outcaste," untouchables, external caste, low class, and pariah.[41] The High Caste people live in Ur as the privileged lot. Pandur Dalits suffered heavily under this cruel system.

2.12.3. Economic

In Pandur village out of total population, 723 were engaged in work activities. 69.85% of workers describe their work as Main Work (Employment or Earning more than 6 Months) while 30.15% were involved in Marginal activity providing livelihood for less than 6 months. Of 723 workers engaged in Main Work, 43 were cultivators (owner or co-owner) while 193 were Agricultural laborers.[42] These figures are from the current statistics but the situation in the early 1900s was very different. Pandur Dalits were landless and jobless laborers and they were very poor economically. Very often famines created the worst disasters among them. It was the Leipzig missionaries who raised their economic status to the present level.

The following incident which was mentioned in the article Johannes Kabis: *Ein Leben für die Mission in Südindien* explains the economic condition of Pandur people in 1900's.

"Once a woman came to Kabis asking him to buy her boy baby for 5 Rupees because she could not feed her baby along her other three children. This she did with the good intention of saving the child. One can imagine their extreme level of poverty."[43] One can imagine their extreme level of poverty.

---

40 V. Devasahayam, "Pollution, Poverty and Powerlessness," in Arvind P. Nirmal (ed) *A Reader in Dalit Theology*, 2.

41 Sathianathan Clarke, Dalit Theology in the Twenty-first century Discordant voices, Discerning pathways, (oxford press: New Delhi), 2010, 5.

42 http://www.census2011.co.in/data/village/629037-Pandur-tamil-nadu.html accessed on 24.2.15.

43 Friedhelm Beyreiss, *Johannes Kabis: Ein Leben für die Mission in Südindien*, (Jever: Sós Éva, Jászszentandrás, 2001), 122. Translated by Lena.

2.12.4. Education

According to Directorate of Census Operations in Tamil Nadu Pandur village has higher literacy rate compared to Tamil Nadu. In 2011, literacy rate of Pandur village was 85.57% compared to 80.09% of Tamil Nadu. In Pandur Male literacy stands at 87.65% while female literacy rate was 83.74%.[44] This is the present situation of Pandur. But in the early days people were uneducated and socially, economically, politically poor. The following statement by a retired teacher will explain how the Pandur population achieved higher literacy rate.

> Mrs. Indrani retired teacher said "my parents are uneducated and *kuli* (Daily wages) but I worked as a government school teacher. She said if Leipzig missionaries didn't come to our village no one will be educated the missionaries started school in Pandur to educate the people who live in and around Pandur."[45]

Next chapter will give detail account how Leipzig mission established the education institute in and around Pandur. Leipzig missionaries strongly believed that only education will uplift the down-trodden.

2.12.5. Religious background

The inhabitants of in and around Pandur villages are basically from Hindu background 77 year old samikanu says:

> My father name is Naraynan his ancestor belongs to Hinduism. His father was a first person who became a Christian.[46]

In the book of *Father of Paria* by Alwin Gehring clearly gives a picture about the religious practices of the people live in and around

44 http://www.census2011.co.in/data/village/629037-Pandur-tamil-nadu.html accessed on 24.2.15.

45 Mrs. Indrani interviewed 18 November 2014 in Kanakaranee.

46 Mr. Samikanu interviewed 17 November 2014 in Pattrai Perrambathur.

Pandur. Kanachawallipuram is one of the neighboring villages to Pandur. The Dalits from the village decided to take baptism so they gave up their idol worship. They worshipped Vishnu and his wife Lakshmi after the baptism the idol fell into complete oblivion.[47]

2.12.6. Mass Conversion

Not only individuals or families in and around Pandur decided to follow Christianity but whole Dalit villages (Mass Conversion) become Christians in and around Pandur.[48] The defining characteristic of the first stage in the modern depressed classes' movement was mass conversion, especially to Christianity, as this was the most dramatic and alarming strap the depressed classes took in the 19th century to improve their lot. This stage may be dated from the 1860s or 1870s through the 1930. The depressed classes themselves took the initiative in conversion. Usually a caste brotherhood or a portion of it in a particular village decided to convert and then encouraged their friends and relatives in neighboring villages to convert as well. This they did because they thought conversion would be a good for their people. Recent studies have indicated that the primary good converts had in mind was not economic (as economic reprisals for outweighed any economic benefits received) but social and psychological: a chance to acquire helpful friends outside the village, and most important of all, these mass conversions were mainly initiated by the Dalits themselves to acquire a new feeling of self-respect, value and dignity.[49] This was the same case in Pandur also because the conversion gave self-respect, value, education and dignity to the Dalits who lived in and around Pandur.

47 Alwin Gehring, *Johannes Kabis Ein Vater der Paria*, 51.

48 Hugald Grafe, *Kirche unter Dalits, Adivasi und Kastenleuten in Südindien* (Berlin: LIT, Publication, 2013), 176.

49 John C. B. Webster, *From Indian Church to Indian Theology: An attempt at Theological Constructio*n, in Arvind P. Nirmal (ed), *A Reader in Dalit Theology* (Chennai: Gurukul Lutheran Theological College & Research Institute, 2007), 97-98.

2.12.7. The background of early Christians in and around Pandur

The Dalits who lived in and around Pandur faced oppression by becoming a Christian. Work and wages were denied, threatened to sue for their debts. It was a difficult time for the Dalit Christians who lived in and around Pandur. When Dalits took baptism, the persecution broke out even more. The Dalit, who came without ashes[50] on the forehead to work, was sent away.[51] Once the *Mirasdar* (High Caste), who was against the Christians, he closed the only spring, where the Paria could get their water. Because, he was the owner of the spring the Christians have to go long distance to take water.[52]

During the time of plague the Christians lost their cattle and there was no work for the Christians' the High Caste man called Christians "Ye fool, what profit you got becoming a Christians? You're God and your Missionary cannot help you. So come back. You shall receive land for lease". This was serious temptation but the Christians remained steadfast in their faith.[53]

50 It denotes the person who has ashes in his forehead is belonging to Hinduism.

51 Alwin Gehring, *Johannes Kabis Ein Vater der Paria*, 58.

52 Beyreiss Fiedhelim, *Johannes Kabis: Ein Leben für die Mission in Südindien*, 20.

53 Alwin Gehring, *Johannes Kabis Ein Vater der Paria,* 50.

Chapter 3

Arrival and Mission Methods of Leipzig Evangelical Lutheran Missionaries

Introduction

This chapter is a brief sketch on the beginning of the Protestant Mission in India, and in and around Pandur. The chapter also reviews the impact of the Christian Missions on the life and conversion of poor Dalits in Pandur area. In and through conversion the Pandur Dalits experienced liberation and transformation. This chapter highlights the methods used by the Leipzig Evangelical Lutheran Mission (LELM), in dealing with Pandur Dalits and the resulting changes including cultural identity of the local people. It is an account of how the depressed communities restored their selfhood through conversion into the Christian faith.

3.1. Protestant Mission in India

On the 29th of November 1705, A.D., Henry Plütschau and Bartholomew Ziegenbalg, left Copenhagen for the East Indies, according to the will of God and on the command of His Majesty

King Fredrick IV of Denmark and Norway, in order to preach the Gospel of Christ to the Gentiles on the Choromandel coast. Thus, begins the first report about the first Lutheran Missionary enterprise in India, one of the first Evangelical Missions in Tamil Nadu. In the 17th centuries Denmark had obtained a number of small colonies in India and among them Tranquebar on the Coromandel Coast, founded in 1620 by the Danish East Indian Company. Until the beginning of the 18th century, however, nothing was done in order to preach the gospel to the Hindus in the colony. In 1699, Fredrik IV came to the Danish throne. Fredrik the IV was a devoted man wished to preach the gospel to the gentiles and he decided to send Missionaries to India.[54]

3.1.1. Arrival of Bartholomew Ziegenbalg and Henry Plütschau

Rev. Bartholomew Ziegenbalg and Henry Plütschau having been ordained in Copenhagen sailed right away to Tranquebar, where they landed on July 9th, 1706. This date was the birth of protestant Missions in India and the Tamil Evangelical Lutheran Church.[55] Almost two hundred years after Martin Luther had begun the Reformation of European Christianity in Germany they had come to be his Evangelical voice to Indians.[56] They didn't get cheerful welcome. King Fredrik had furnished them with a royal warrant of legal representative and a letter of recommendation to the governor of the colony; but he had forgotten to consult with the mighty East Indian Company, which was absolutely against any Missionary enterprise in their colonies.[57] Ziegenbalg and Plütschau had not come to Tranquebar to serve the Europeans or to study India. Their main goal was to bear witness to the gospel of Jesus Christ among

54 Sigfrid Estborn, "The Tranquebar Mission" in C.H. Swavely (ed) *Lutheran Enterprises in India,* 1706-1952 (Madras: Federation of Evangelical Lutheran Churches in India, 1952), 1.

55 Ibid., 2.

56 Dennis Hudson, *Protestant Origins in India: Tamil Evangelical Christians,* 1707-1835 (Richmond, Surrey: William B. Eerdmans Publishing & Co, 2000), 1.

57 Sigfrid Estborn, "The Tranquebar Mission" in C.H. Swavely (ed) *Lutheran Enterprises in India,* 1706-1952, 2.

the Gentiles by words and deeds. They were the first Europeans sent to India for that purpose. After the arrival of Ziegenbalg and Plütschau, other three Germans, namely J. E. Gruendler, P. Jordan, and J. G. Boveingh, came to Tranquebar. Over the next 131 years of the Danish-Halle Mission, 51 other Europeans would continue what they had begun.[58]

3.1.2. Dark period of Halle Mission

After the death of Schwartz[59] in 1798 the Tranquebar Mission which had already been suffering a decline almost became defunct. The real cause of this decline is scarcely to be found in the wars and the political confusion of the time, nor in the co-operation of the Lutherans and the Anglicans, which now and then had caused some confessional controversies, but in the inner conditions of the home-Churches, although called into existence by a Danish initiative the Tranquebar Mission had never been embraced with real interest by the Danish Church. The heart of the Mission was Halle.[60]

The Missionary zeal started to decline in Germany. The German Churches took little importance in the Mission, and even though the orthodox criticism slowly disappeared, the Churches remained, on the whole, indifferent. But towards the close of the 18th century the old ardent spirit of pietism was dying out.[61] According to Rev. Sigfrid Estborn said "the leaders of Halle lost their first love. The rationalism and Neology entered into the Church, and they were by no means favorable to Missions. A relativism, which regarded all religions as the same value could not promote a passionate Missionary

58 Dennis Hudson, *Protestant Origins in India: Tamil Evangelical Christians, 1707-1835,* 10.

59 Christian friedrich Schwartz was born in Poland in 1726. Ordained in Copenhagen in 1749, he arrived in India in1750 as a Lutheran Missionary. He worked in Tranquebar, Trichy and Tanjore for forty eight years without returning to his home country. While in India, Schwartz learned Tamil, Telugu, Sanskrit, Persian, Hindustani, Marathi and Portuguese, and he assisted translation of the bible into Tamil.

60 R. Handmann, Die Ev. Luth. Tamulen Mission (Leipzig, 1903), 23.

61 Sigfrid Estborn, "The Tranquebar Mission" in C. H. Swavely (ed) *Lutheran Enterprises in India*, 1706-1952, 13.

spirit. The leaders from Halle complained it's become more difficult to find young men who are ready to go out as Missionaries. The Copenhagen the Mission was ridiculed and the secretary of the collegiums expressed his definite opposition against conversions of Hindus to Christianity."[62]

As we seen above the wave of rationalism which entered into European churches and swept over the interest in Missions almost died out. The Missionaries towards the end received great support for their work from England. It was natural that English societies should send English Missionaries, and so the Anglican Missions largely reaped the fruits of the labors of the Danish-Halle Missionaries.[63]

3.2. Anglican Period

Great awakening of the Missionary spirit in England emerged. It was therefore only in result of the development that had taken place, that Kemmerer, the last of the Tranquebar Missionaries, in 1820, handed over the S.P.C.K.[64] 1,300 Christians, 11 catechists and 11 small churches along with their property, as these Christians were English subjects in the province of Tanjore. When the society for the propagation of the Gospel (S.P.G), in 1825, took over the S.P.C.K. its Mission in India, all stations supported by English money, beside with their congregations and Missions agents were integrated into the Anglican Church. Now only Tranquebar remained, and this colony was sold to England in 1844, on the condition, however, that the congregation there should remain Lutheran. Those congregations which had been incorporated in the Anglican Church were afterwards shaken by the terrible cast-controversy. The Anglicans were much more radical in regard to caste than the Tranquebar fathers, who stressed that caste, should be discarded immediately, decidedly and

62 Sigfrid Estborn, "The Tranquebar Mission" in C. H. Swavely (ed) *Lutheran Enterprises in India*, 1706-1952, 13.

63 L. B. Wolf, (Ed) *Missionary Heroes of the Lutheran Church* (Philadelphia: The Lutheran Publication Society, 1911), 64.

64 The Society for Promoting Christian Knowledge (SPCK) is the oldest Anglican Mission organization. It was Originate in 1698 by Thomas Bray (an Anglican Priest), and a small group of friends. The most important Early leaders were Anton Wilhelm Boehm and court preacher Friedrich Michael Ziegenhagen.

definitely. This extremism pricked the strong caste feelings of the old Lutheran shudras. Many went away from the Anglican Church and some went back to Hinduism. But, at that time another Mission stood ready to take care of the Lutheran heritage in India.[65]

3.3. Leipzig Evangelical Lutheran Mission

It will be hard to discover periods in the history of Missions which are to be equaled to the time of decay and disaster forming the end of the history of the Tranquebar Mission. At the beginning of the nineteenth century the blessed, prosperous, and promising work done by that Mission had suffered an unparalleled setback caused chiefly by the torrent of rationalism which swept Europe and by the imprudent tactics of those who were absorbing the remnants of the Tranquebar Mission. A aloof home-board, castrated stations, congregations diminishing in number, bad decaying in spiritual and moral life and Missionaries left in a hopeless position and therefore willing to let matters drift were the reasons end of the Tranquebar Mission. No doubt any successor to step into this work, finds a heritage with fixed obligations. Roads are already laid out, and though they may be in a bad condition, the line of March is to be adjusted accordingly. This was the real condition of Tranquebar Mission when LELM Mission took control over Tranquebar Mission.[66]

3.3.1. History of Leipzig Mission

The Leipzig Evangelical Lutheran Mission was founded on August 17, 1836. She developed from a Mission society which mainly supported the Basel Mission. The desire of Lutheran Mission was understood on the part of the Basel Mission. The foremost task of the newly founded Mission was then to find the appropriate field for her activities.[67]

---

65 Sigfrid Estborn, "The Tranquebar Mission" in C. H. Swavely (ed.) *The Lutheran Enterprise in India,* 13.

66 W. Hellinger, "The Leipzig Evangelical Lutheran Mission" in C. H. Swavely (ed.) *Lutheran Enterprises in India*, 1706-1952, 15.

67 Ibid., 15.

The society was established at Dresden on the 16th of August, 1819. A preparatory school for Missionary candidates was opened in 1832, but it was not until 1836 that the society began Missionary operations as such. In 1848, its central scat was removed from Dresden to Leipzig in order that the Mission students might have the benefit of the university education: at the same time the society received its present organization and its title was changed from Dresden to Leipzig society.[68]

3.3.2. Leipzig Mission in India

The foremost task of the newly founded Mission was then to find a suitable field for her activities. Even though, several works had been begun in Australia, it was felt, that position of the Tranquebar Mission imposed an obligation on Lutheran churches and that it was a responsibility of love to respond to that obligation. I.H.C. Cordes was sent to India to investigate the situation at close quarters. He arrived December on 27, 1840 in Madras and on March 20, 1841 in Tranquebar. The Danish pastor Kundson in Tranquebar, who though ailing, sincerely tried to improve matters there, welcomed Cordes heartily. Both became friends very soon and as early as 1842 he got permission from Danish governor to found a Teachers Training school in *Poryar,* this training school played a vital role in Leipzig Mission while establishing schools in the Mission fields, the teachers were trained and sent to different LELM stations. After the arrival of H.C. Cordes two other Missionaries arrived at Tamil Nadu from Leipzig namely C.E.C. Ochas in 1842 and T.M.N. Schwartz in 1843.[69]

Following them many Missionaries came to India especially to Tamil Nadu from LELM and worked in different Mission stations. One of the largest Mission stations of LELM was Pandur. The next section will give a detailed account of the Missionaries and their work in and around Pandur.

---

68 B. H. Badley, *Indian Missionary Directory and Memorial Volume* (Lucknow: American Methodist Mission, 1876), 177.

69 W. Hellinger "The Leipzig Evangelical Lutheran Mission" in C. H. Swavely. (ed) *The Lutheran Enterprise in* India, 15-16.

3.4. Leipzig Missionaries in Pandur

It was the Missionary Kabis from Madras who had evangelized the area of Pandur around 1890.[70] In 1893, he was posted in Thiruvallur station. Pandur was under Thiruvallur pastorate in the beginning when he started his Mission work among villages. Pandur was one among the villages then. He bifurcated Pandur as a separate pastorate. From 1893 till 1990 there were 12 Missionaries from Europe who did Mission work in and around Pandur, four from Sweden and eight from Germany. According to the Annual Report of Leipzig Mission in 1932, Pandur became the second largest Mission station. There were 1300 Christian living in and around Pandur. A brief account of the Missionaries who worked in around Pandur is given below.

3.4.1. Rev. Johannes Kabis

Johannes Kabis, born on August 1, 1853 in Rudolstadt, entered the Leipzig Mission seminar October 1868. He studied theology and was reassigned on May 23, 1877, after India. Over time he worked at different stations (Madras, Mayavaram, Chingleput, Bangalore and Pandur), founded the station Tiruvallur. Kabis married Torah Riemer from Cologne on November 25, 1879 in Madras. 32 years he worked under the Tamil in the vicinity of Madras (1877-1909). In Pandur he worked from 1893 to 1907. Till 1910 he worked in India. Due to his health condition, he returned to Germany and he lived in Hamburg and he died on March 30, 1919.[71]

3.4.2. Rev. Rudolf Enno Schomerus

Born on September 16, 1869 in Marienhafe in East friesland, studied in the Leipzig Seminary, was ordained at Hannover 10th May, 1891; he arrived in India on 26th September 1891, in 1907, he arrived at

70 J. W. Ruckdaeschel, *1911-1916 Missionar der Evangelical Lutheran Leipziger Heiden Mission auf der Station Pandur bei Madras in Südindien*, unpublished material, 4. Translated by J. R. Jayabalan.

71 http://www.lmw-Mission.de/de/Missionar-13.html accessed on 27-03-2015.

Pandur with his wife and two children. 1891 and died at Pandur 9th April 1913[72] due to typhoid.[73]

3.4.3. Rev. Elias Soederstroem

Born on 1886 he was ordained on 1920 and he arrived in India in 1921, worked in Pudukkotai, Pattukotai and Pandur. From 1921 to 1927 he worked in Pandur due to his health condition he returned to Germany in 1927.[74]

3.4.4. Rev. Karl Heller

Karl Heller was born on 26 December 1885 in Leisnig, Germany as the son of a merchant. From 1907 to 1908, he was teaching vicar in Oberaltertheim in Lower Franconia. On June 10, 1908, he was sent to South India (now Tamil Nadu) seconded and stationed at Cuddalore. Heller was commissioned in the spring of 1911 led the industrial school in Erukatantscheri, in autumn 1912 he became head of the station Chidambaram. After the outbreak of the First World War, he was interned early January 1916 in Ahmednagar. In the spring of 1916, he returned to Germany and worked from 1920 as a priest as Vicar in Zwota. In 1927, he traveled to India and took over the station Pandur. There, he took care of the agricultural autonomy (scheduled castes) small tenants, digged well and a small hospital. A big help was always his wife Selma. 1955 he returned to Germany, where he worked in Bavaria. Karl Heller died on September 6, 1966 in the Feierabendhaus the Rummel Berger institutions.[75]

3.4.5. Rev. Wilhelm Ruckdaeschel

Johannes Wilhelm Ruckdaeschel was born on February 2, 1887 in White City, Bavaria, as the son of a stone-machine grinder. On October 23, 1910, he arrived to India as a Missionary in Pandur. But during this time Missionary Kannegiesser went to holiday to

---

72 Catherine Vimala, *Pandur in Tranquebar Mission History*, 31-32.

73 http://www.lmw-Mission.de/de/Missionar-126.html accessed on 27.3.2015.

74 Samuel Iyyer, *History of Tranquebar Mission* (Madras: The Tranquebar Printing & Publishing House, 1955), 247.

75 http://www.lmw-Mission.de/de/Missionar-187.html accessed on 27.3.2015.

Germany so he served in Thiruvallur 1912-1913.then he served in Pandur from May 1913 to November 1914. After the outbreak of the First World War, he was a prisoner of war in Chennai and Ahmednagar from October 1914 until March 1916. He went back to Germany and April 11, 1973 in his home town of white city in Upper Franconia.[76]

3.4.6. Rev. Karl Kannegiesser

Born at Madras, India 8th March 1909 son of Missionary Georg Kannegiesser studied agriculture at Witzenhausen, Germany and got the diploma for farming in tropical countries, arrived in Colombo 22nd February, 1932, stationed at Pandur as administrator of Pandur farms, during his period in Pandur he developed the rice field with his experience. Then he returned to Germany on furlough May 1938, but could not go back to India due to the outbreak of war, became inspector of economy at Kronsbergfarm, Hannover- wülfel[77] he died on 12 May 1985.[78]

3.4.7. Miss Elisabeth Buchholz

Born in Göttingen 30th March 1909, studied Theology arrived in India 31st January, 1938, stationed at Madras and Pandur, repatriated after outbreak of war February, 1940, entered church-service in Hessen.

3.4.8. Sister Johanna Zimmermann

Born at Chemnitz 27th January, 1902, became nurse and deaconess in diakonissenhaus Dresden, arrived in Colombo 29th February, 1936, stationed at Mayavaram. In 1937,[79] she passed the first Tamil language exams. In February 1938, she was the second Tamil language exams in Tranquebar and then took over the hospital work independently in Pandur Hospital, due to war had to leave India on

76 Samuel Iyyer, *History of Tranquebar Mission*, 238.

77 Ibid., 242.

78 http://www.lmw-Mission.de/de/Missionar-226.html accessed on 30.3.15.

79 Samuel Iyyer, *History of Tranquebar Mission*, 254.

1940[80] again she came to India on 1950 September 6th she worked in Chennai and Mayavaram she went back to Germany in 1964 She died in Dresden on April 27, 1980.[81]

3.4.9. Rev. Hans Woxblom

He was born in Sweden in 1904, ordained in 1927 he arrived to India in 1935 he served in different Mission station in Tamil Nadu during the war the German Missionaries were sent out of India during that time Rev. H. Woxblorn worked in Pandur in the between 1940 to 1942.[82]

3.4.10. Miss Marie Haback

She was Born on 1894 in Sweden, 1924 she was sent to India, the Danish Mission from 1924 to 1948 she worked for Sweden Mission. 1940 she came to Tamil Nadu and worked in different places in Tamil Nadu from 1942 to 1948 she worked in Pandur. In 1948, she gave the station to Heller came back to India and he worked until 1955.[83]

3.4.11. Luise Fröhlich

She was born on 30th April 1902 in Tranquebar India as the daughter of a Missionary Dr. Richard Froehlich. Her father was a lecturer at the Gurukul College in Chennai. In April 1905, she went back to Germany for education. She return back on 10 January 1928; entered Mission service. In 1930, she took the place of sister Magdalene Matthes during her furlough in LELM Girls school at Madras. Then she worked in Pandur from 1935 to 1938 and went back to Germany on February 1940 remained in Mission-home service again she returned to India 15th March, 1951, stationed at Kumabakonam until August 1955. From 1955 to 1967 she worked in Pandur specially worked among the Dalit women in and around Pandur. During her period in Pandur she played a vital role to uplift

---

80 Catherine Vimala, *Pandur in Tranquebar Mission History*, 41.

81 http://www.lmw-Mission.de/de/Missionar-237.html accessed on 30.3.2015.

82 Catherine Vimala, *Pandur in Tranquebar Mission History*, 42.

83 Ibid., 43.

the Dalit women and children she constructed a new building for girls home and named froelich girls home. She has supported many poor children for their education till now some of them are alive they are in good position. Luise Fröhlich died on 11 May 1989.[84]

3.4.12. Silesia Lüben Ruhnke Lydia

She was born in 14th November 1929. After attending school and catechists seminar took on an apprenticeship as a nurse at the Deaconess Motherhouse in Eisenach, in 1951 with "very good" grade. Her desire was to work abroad as a deaconess; in 1959 she studied in Leipzig Mission House. On 26 June 1962 she went to England and learned English then she was consecrated as a Missionary to India She was stationed in Pandur and Thanjavur to learn Tamil language. At first she was head of the Elementary High School in Thanjavur for the upbringing, education and health of children responsible (girls aged 8 to 18 years). She took over in 1968 as head of the girls' boarding school in Pandur.[85] During her period in Pandur she developed the medical work especially for the pregnant ladies she brought the experienced doctors from nearby hospital in ikaddu and gave treatment for the pregnant women. She raised fund to reconstructed the Kabis Higher secondary school in 1975 the new school building was constructed.[86] Due to her health condition she went back to Germany 2.9.1990 and she died on July 2, 2016.[87]

3.5. Mission Methods of Leipzig Mission Societies

Its focus is on how the Dalits have sourced various social, economic and political resources from the dissenting peripheries and marginal cultural traditions of socio-religious reform movements to construct a new community identity, reconstruct a cultural history, and invent a liberation ideology. From a subjugated position of 'outcastes' in the caste hierarchy, the contemporary Dalits have deployed various mobility strategies to overcome caste inequality and oppression to

84 Catherine Vimala, *Pandur in Tranquebar Mission History,* 45.

85 http://www.lmw-Mission.de/de/Missionar-253.html accessed on 30.3.15.

86 Catherine Vimala, *Pandur in Tranquebar Mission History,* 46.

87 https://www.lmw-mission.de/Missionar-150.html accessed on 4.3.2017.

achieve social, economic mobility and political power. Multipronged Mission methods of social and economic mobility through education, medical work and employment facilitated the identity assertion and thereby resulted in creation of politico-cultural liberation ideology that gained a global visibility and essentially defines the Dalits in and around Pandur.

3.5.1. Education

> Mr. Samraj said "the upper caste people did not like that the Dalit should be educated because if Dalit got education then who would do the menial jobs in their homes. So high caste people always kept Dalits in and around Pandur uneducated and used them to do menial jobs in their homes and farms. And another reason was there was no school in and around Pandur. To educate their children parents must take them Thiruvallur which was far away from Pandur."[88]

Due to these reasons the people who are in and around Pandur were uneducated in 1900's. Then Kabis realized that education could empower the people and so he started the elementary school in 1904 and it was recognized by the government in 1920.[89] During that time there were 28 children - 20 boys and 8 girls in Pandur. The basics were taught for children, i.e., English alphabets, Tamil alphabets and they learned 1-100 numbers and along with this the Bible also was taught to the children.[90]

Rev. Heller took effort to bring up the level of the school. Then he raised the level of education from elementary to secondary school in 1928. With the help of some local teachers such as Mr. Moses, Mr. Devasagahyam, Mr. Arumai Nayagam and Mr. Jesupatham, etc. the School became the Higher Secondary School in 1966. In 1975, sister Lydia Runke raised fund and constructed new school building.[91]

---

88 Mr. Samraj interviewed 18 November 2014 in Kanakaranee.

89 Catherine Vimala, *Pandur in Tranquebar Mission History*, 54.

90 Johannes Kabis, *Palmzweige aus dem ostindischen Missionfelde* (Leipzig: Verlag der Evanglical Lutheran Mission, 1898), 25. Transalted by Irene Heinke.

91 Catherine Vimala, *Pandur in Tranquebar Mission History*, 58.

3.5.2. Sewing school

Missionary Kabis and his wife strongly believed that sewing training could help the women who lived in and around Pandur and help them earn some money and job opportunity. (see: Appendix C: Sewing School)

The sewing school started with a little girl from Pandur karnei and it was promoted to other girls and women in and around Pandur. In the beginning only few decided to learn sewing. These children had even no idea about sewing. There is only one woman in the village, who reached the sewing level. Kabis, his wife and daughter Martha taught Sudra and pariah girls how to sew. Very few Sudra girls came from Thiruvallur but the Christian pariah girls were numerous. These Girls were eager to learn sewing which made them very happy. These girls sewed skirts, rocket, and others items. They were happy when they sewed bags.[92] The sewing school in Pandur was able to mend torn dresses.[93]

Because of the sewing school only, the sewing school students had clothes up to the hips. Only the teachers' and catechist's children were somewhat better dressed, with skirts, and blouses. The girls would come on Christmas to get skirts; this was their request always. The sewing school is crowded at the moment and some girls learned a lot already.[94]

After Kabis Rev. Schomerus wife Gesina took charge and taught the girls bobbin lace-making. The girls learned and they developed very fast. Rudolf wrote in his last report which was published after his death "The lace making school is now well established. Several girls have earned enough to cover their wedding costs and also found that their earning very valuable to their families. The lace was then sent to Germany where it was sold in the home communities.[95]

In 1977, January 2nd the sewing school was renovated by sister Lydia Runke and she appointed Mrs. Catharine Vimala Devaraj as

92 Friedhelm Beyreiss, *Johannes Kabis: Ein Leben für die Mission in Südindien*,125-126.

93 Ibid., 125-126.

94 Ibid., 123-124.

95 http://www.amycarmichel.bplaced.net/Rudolf_Schomerus.pdf, 6.

supervisor and two sewing teachers were appointed to teach sewing to the poor girls who are in and around Pandur. 12th October 1980 the new building was built and inaugurated. A lot of female students are trained in this school and sent to the government exams. After they get the certificate many students are self employed. By stitching dress they get money for their daily living.[96]

3.5.3. Girls Hostel

In 1951, Missionary Heller started the boarding school for girls Rev. Heller named the boarding home as a *kesthena Sthalam*. To start with 10 girls joined the home. Rev. Heller's wife Mrs. Selma was taking care of the 10 girls and the boarding home. Later this home got support from the government. Later Missionary Froelich expanded this home and named Froelich Girls Hostel. The girls who study in this hostel after the school education they would be sent for a higher education such as teacher training, nursing, etc. Froelich Home helped a lot of poor Dalit girls who are in and around Pandur to get education and attain a good level in the society.[97]

3.5.4. Heller Boys Hostel

In 1904, the boy's hostel was started by Kabis. In the earlier stages the hostel was supported by the German Mission. Later Rev. Heller took interest and in 1930 the government started to support the Boys Hostel. Dalit Boys who lived in and around Pandur stayed in the hostel and studied in Kabis School. After their school education they were sent for higher studies such as Teacher training, Nursing, Arts, ITI etc… it helped them to attain good level in the society.[98]

3.5.5. Kindergarten

Anbu Illam this is the name of the kindergarten started by sister Lydia Runcke on 12th October 1982. Here, they provide healthy food and vitamin tablets for the children. Basically it was started to help the working parents. During the day time the children were at home and

96 Catherine Vimala, Pandur *in Tranquebar Mission History*, 58.

97 Ibid., 57.

98 Ibid., 55.

the parents felt insecure. This home helped the parents to go to work without any worry about their children.[99]

3.5.6. Medical work

The villages in and around Pandur do not have transport facilities. If someone fell sick he/she must to go Thiruvallur for treatment. Without transport facilities it was very difficult for person to reach Thiruvallur. When Rev. Heller saw the difficulties of the people he decided to start a clinic in Pandur. March 23 1930 the clinic was inaugurated by the Missionary Heller. Sister Magdalene Matthes[100] was the in charge for the clinic and with the help of educated bible woman from the pariah caste. They treated several sick people who lived in and around Pandur. The sick people from in and around Pandur came to the clinic and got treatment for their sickness and were cured. This clinic is not only for pariahs but also for all the caste people.[101] People who are in and around Pandur suffered various kinds of diseases. Predominantly children had worm diseases and others suffered from pestering wounds, ulcers and rashes with dysenteries, malaria, kidney infections, etc. Missionaries Heller and sister Magdalene Matthes took care and treated these people and the people got cured from their diseases. The small clinic was a great blessing for the people who lived in and around Pandur.

3.5.7. Distributions of land

The Dalits who lived in and around Pandur were landless laborers. Not only in Pandur but all over India in 1900 Dalits were landless

99 Catherine Vimala, *Pandur in Tranquebar Mission History*, 59.

100 Sister of Magdalene Matthes was born on September 4, 1892, in Tranquebar as the daughter of Missionary of Macdonald. She attended the Higher school for young ladies in Neuendettelsau, Dresden and the manual work teacher seminar in Himmelkron. After she had passed the exam in Bayreuth, she worked as a teacher in Himmelskron and Nördlingen. Then she joined the Deaconess House in Neuendettelsau and took the State exam for nursing in 1926. After she had taken part in the sister course in the Mission home, she was reassigned on October 24, 1927, after India. She landed in Colombo on December 2, 1927. From 1927 to 1930, she was in Mayavaram, then in Pandur and 1931 to 1935 in Madras.

101 Catherine Vimala, *Pandur in Tranquebar Mission History*, 56.

laborers; they worked as daily laborers under the upper caste people. The land owners exploited the Dalits.

According to Hellinger rural settlements on a larger scale were founded by Kabis near Trivellore and Pandur. Large plots of land were purchased, cultivated and leased out to the members of the flourishing congregation there. The end in view was to make the villagers economically independent.[102]

Let us see how Johannes Kabis purchased land and disturbed to the Dalits who lived in and around Pandur.

A Brahmin widow in Kanachawallipuram wanted to sell her lands, which was leased by a man called Kuppusami. Now Kabis was keen to purchase of such property. But the church in Tranquebar was quiet unwilling to give him permission. But Kabis took the bold decision to buy the land for the sake of poor Christians who are always working as laborers under the upper caste people without good salary.[103] Finally, He succeeded and purchased the land with the help of his friend in Dresden for 2000 Marks. Kabis didn't buy directly the land from the Brahmin widow. A middleman bought the land from the Brahmin widow and sold to the Mission, for the Brahman widow was not willing to sell her property to the Missionaries. Later the Brahmin widow came to know that the land was bought by the Missionaries. She got angry shouting and cursing Christian Missions. The rice land leased to the Christian pariahs. The tenant paid the rent money in spices, in rice, and it was the Christian Missionary who helped with it. Now, the Missionary of Pandur was bread giver to many people, and as such he was highly regarded and respected.[104]

3.5.8. Voice for the voice less

The high caste landowner claimed the land belonged to two small pariah farmers. He filed a case against those two small farmers and

102 W. Hellinger, "The Leipzig Evangelical Lutheran Mission" in C.H. Swavely (ed) *The Lutheran Enterprise in India,* 21.

103 Alwin Gehring, *Johannes Kabis: A Father of Pariah,* 50.

104 J.W. Ruckdaeschel, *1911-1916 Missionar der Evangelical Lutheran Leipziger HeidenMission auf der Station Pandur bei Madras in Südindien,* unpublished material, 7.

tried to grab the land from the pariah farmers. The judge who was dealing with the case was a Brahmin and the landowner also was a Brahmin. A Brahmin will never harm a Brahmin. So, the pariah farmers knew for sure that the judgment would be in favor of the Brahmin. So, they went to Johannes Kabis and asked him to be present in the court and support the poor farmers; for when the white man appeared surely the judge could not do favor for a Brahmin in front of white man. Johannes Kabis was present on the trial and the poor farmer got justice. The land was given back to the poor pariah family.[105]

3.5.9. Agricultural school

Kabis established agricultural school and carpentry and brought iron for the use of Farmers. National foundation from Germany gave him 20,000 marks to start the school. But due to the war the school was closed lack of supervision.[106]

In the agriculture school, they trained young people in Pandur for agriculture, and gave them practical training, especially to teach them how to use the wind engine which pumped the water from the well in to a pool and fields. Through this well and wind engine they showed the people in Pandur that a triple harvest is possible.[107]

3.5.10. Cemetery

Pandur lacked cemetery, the Christians buried their dead in the burning space acquired by the Hindus.[108] Johannes Kabis purchased a suitable property which is easily accessible for four Christian villages. November 29, 1905 was the first burial it was also the day of dedication of the cemetery. The first seed that was placed in this

105 J.W. Ruckdaeschel, *1911-1916 Missionar der Evangelical Lutheran Leipziger HeidenMission auf der Station Pandur bei Madras in Südindien,* unpublished material, 6.

106 Alwin Gehring, *Johannes Kabis: A Father of Pariah,* 69.

107 J.W. Ruckdaeschel, *1911-1916 Missionar der Evangelical Lutheran Leipziger HeidenMission auf der Station Pandur bei Madras in Südindien,* unpublished material, 35.

108 Friedhelm Beyreiss, *Johannes Kabis: Ein Leben für die Mission in Südindien,* 129.

cemetery in this world, was a devout young girl named *Jesu Pillai* (Child of Jesus). When Kabis in the evening of that day made his usual diary quotations, he found that November 29th was the day on which 200 years ago Ziegenbalg with Plütschau from Copenhagen assumed their trip to India. This gave him the idea to build a nice big cross in the cemetery of Pandur in memory of the anniversary celebration of the Lutheran Mission in India. A granite stone from the ruined temple of Pandur should serve as a base and was elaborately polished and coated with an appropriate inscription. On Easter morning the cemetery cross was unveiled. Kabis conducted a service in the Cemetery. It was decided to repeat the celebration every year at the cemetery.[109]

3.5.11. Well

Missionary Rev. Wilhelm Ruckdaeschel Beautiful explained how well and water is important in India.

Europeans cannot understand what a well with plenty of water in India, because Europeans do not know even the lack of water, the India threatened almost continuously. In India, water was not just water, it was also food- rice independent from the rain hope for an easier and better and more beautiful life.[110]

When Missionaries arrived in the Mission field and a site was bought, the first thought was digging a well. Good water is the basic condition for a new station. Digging well is not only for building but also to help the Christians do agriculture during the time of water crisis. During the time of famine order was given to excavate the well in Wideiur. Christians from the village were thankful to the Mission.[111]

During the time of famine all over Tamil Nadu people are suffering without rain and it created starvation. But, LELM Mission station Pandur and the three neighboring villages had a well to do agriculture. Day and night people from in and around Pandur used

109 Alwin Gehring, *Johannes Kabis: A Father of Pariah*, 69-70.

110 J.W. Ruckdaeschel, *1911-1916 Missionar der Evangelical Lutheran Leipziger HeidenMission auf der Station Pandur bei Madras in Südindien,* unpublished material, 34.

111 Alwin Gehring, *Johannes Kabis: A Father of Pariah*, 62.

the well. People from other villages came to Kabis and asked help from him. They asked him to dig well for their village too. With the help of a Missionary friend Johannes Kabis dug a lot of wells. Due to this hundreds of people got employment.[112] In Kanachawallipuram, four new large deep wells were dug and that created job opportunities for many Christians.[113]

3.6. Evangelistic Work

The LELM did evangelistic work where ever it was possible but the continuous increase in the number of stations necessitated so much educational, pastoral and administrative work, that the number of workers available was insufficient for even this work which pressed itself to the foreground. It happened rarely that a Missionary could devote his time solely to evangelistic work. Still there was a steady increase in the number of souls. In 1860, there were 4846 souls; in 1885 the congregations consisted of 13,720 souls. In 1913, the number of the souls increased to 22,033. But this increase does not correspond to the number of the converts and children baptized.[114]

Sometimes it was suggested to limit the field to a smaller area in order to do more concentrated work, whereby time and efforts could have been spared for evangelization. But circumstances did not show a practical way and so evangelistic work remained an activity among others.[115] Only a few Missionaries had the privilege to devote their time to evangelism and social work balancing both properly. Missionary Kabis visited the villages and preached the Gospel. On 31.12.1893 he gave baptism for 42 converts, and on 18.11.1894 he gave baptism for 62 new converts in kanakaranee.[116] 43 first fruits in Pandur were baptized on 12th July, 1895[117] Later

112 Alwin Gehring, *Johannes Kabis: A Father of Pariah*, 66.

113 Friedhelm Beyreiss, *Johannes Kabis: Ein Leben für die Mission in Südindien*, 121.

114 W. Hellinger. "*The Leipzig Evangelical Lutheran Mission*" in C.H. Swavely (ed) *The Lutheran Enterprise in India*, 20.

115 Ibid., 20.

116 Catherine Vimala, Pandur *in Tranquebar Mission History*, 25.

117 Johannes Kabis, *Palmzweige aus ostindischen Missionsfelde*, Transalted by Rev. Irene Heinke, 12.

his successor also evangelized people in and around Pandur. Once Rev. Schomerus when was working in Pandur traveled to a nearby place called *Pariyapalayam* a Hindu pilgrimage centre. He saw people worshiping idols without dress. This ignorance of the people disturbed him and he started to preach the gospel and many people became Christians.[118] During the period of Luise Florich weekly once she would go to Pandur in a bullock cart and preach the gospel to the people around the village.[119]

3.6.1. Church planting

Leipzig Missionaries, where ever they established a congregation they planted churches. In Pandur, in the beginning they did not have a church but the first baptism took place in cow shed where people gathered and worshipped. But later Kabis bought a small place and built a small chapel but it was not enough. Members increased. Kabis and his wife felt that they needed a big church. Rev. Kabis wrote letters to the old friends in Germany and they sent money to him for that project. The German congregation raised funds by selling their left over crops after their harvest and that is why Kabis named the church as *Kadhir Alayam- Kadhir* means crop and *Alayam* means church (see: Appendix C: Photo of Pandur Kadhirallayam).[120]

Kabis laid the foundation stone in August 1906. The construction began at once but Rev. Kabis could not finish it. He became ill he had to leave Pandur and to live and to work in Bangalore where the climate is much better. So it was his successor Rev. Schomerus who finished the building. In spring 1908 from 31.12.1908 to 06.01.1909 thanksgiving service for the new church was held. On 06.01.1909 Kabis and his family came to Pandur and consecrated the new church. The great altar picture was donated by a German princess *Thekla* from *Schwarzburg-Rudolstadt.*[121]

Till today this church is a blessing for the people who live in and around Pandur. Every Sunday more than 400 people assemble

118 Catherine Vimala, *Pandur in Tranquebar Mission History*, 32.

119 Ibid., 45.

120 Ibid., 29.

121 Ibid., 30.

for the Sunday service. The church is packed even today. People do not have place to sit inside the church. The church is open and everyday people who live in and around Pandur come and pray and light candles.

3.6.2. Catechumens

Johannes Kabis was looking after all these congregations and the schools he established. Whenever a group of people expressed interest in becoming Christians, they were given instruction and treated as catechumens. When the Missionaries were convinced that the catechumens were genuinely interested and had received sufficient training then in the presence of the congregation the catechumens were examined and then they were baptized. They were accepted as communicants. Once Kabis asked a question to catechumens, "Have you renounced the devil and work of devil?" The old man innocently replied why do you ask for that which I had given up already four months ago?[122]

After the failure of the Halle Mission in India as we seen above the LELM took over and they stated to flourish both in Spiritual and social work in Tamil Nadu especially in Pandur. The World War created problem to German Mission societies in India let us see how war intervene the LELM and how they overcame these problem.

3.7. Intervention of war

The greatest reverse the work of the LELM. Suffered was caused by the great war of 1914-1918. When the war broke out the German Missionaries were allowed continue their work. The Governor of Madras and leading English Missionaries rendered them the help they could. But soon the situation changed and by April 1916 all German Missionaries were interned and send back.[123]

In those times of political change, Missionaries were put under closer watch by the government. Non-British nationals were affected first. It is not known, whether a severe critique of British colonial

122 Alwin Gehring, *Johannes Kabis: A Father of Pariah,* 49.

123 W. Hellinger, "*The Leipzig Evangelical Lutheran Mission*" in C. H. Swavely (ed) *The Lutheran Enterprise in India,* 26.

policies in India by a former German Indian Missionary on the staff of LELM at Leipzig presented to an international Missionary conference at Uppsala. Before the World War I, ever came to the knowledge of British authorities. But throughout the war all German Missionaries were looked upon enemies of the empire, were interned, sent back to Germany by 1916, and none of their group was allowed to return before 1925.[124]

The First World War which took place between 1914-1918 brought in a change in the relationship between the state and the church. Germany and Great Britain were in opposite camps during this war. When the war was going on, the British government began to restrict the activities and the entry of non-British Missionaries in her colonies which were under her rule. The non-British Missionaries who were already working in India and those who wished to come into India were required to obtain permits from the British government. Letters and other communications were censored. Such restrictions came into operations from 1916.[125]

Soon after the First World War broke out, the German and Austrian Missionaries in India, both Protestants and Roman Catholics were asked to register at the office of the District commissioners or district Collectors as the case may be. They were asked to sign a document saying that they would not do anything to damage the interests of the British Government. They were required to surrender to the government whatever arms and ammunitions they possessed. Their movements were restricted. Their mails were scrutinized.[126]

3.8. Swedish Mission in India

In 1916, the work of the Leipzig Evangelical Lutheran Mission and its properties in Tamil Nadu were transferred to the Church of Sweden

---

124 Hugald Grafe, *History of Christianity in Tamil Nadu from 1800 to1975*, 233.

125 D. Arthur Jeyakumar, *Bishop Johannes Sandegren and the British Government of India*, Indian Church History Review (Mumbai: Indian Church History Review, Vol. XXX, Number 1, June 1996), 6.

126 Carl Becker, *History of the Catholic Missions in North East India,* 1890-1915 (Shillong: Firma KLM, 1980), 342.

Mission.[127] Rev. Meyner written to the government office says the Leipzig Mission is handling over their Proporities and Institutions.

"We (Leipzig Mission) have the honor to inform you (British Government) that, on the 15th Sept. 1915, the home board of the LELM decided to withdraw from Mission work in India and to hand over unconditionally to the church of Sweden Mission board at Stockholm the administration of Mission work in India with all its properties and institutions. This transfer intended to take effect from the moment the German Missionaries are removed from their stations, and the Rev. D. Bexell, the secretary of the church of Sweden Mission, will become the head of the whole Mission, i.e., church of Sweden Mission together with the hitherto existing LELM."[128] Four Russians were nominated to supervise the work of Sweden Mission.[129] These Russians basically Germans but technically Russian citizens.[130] The Swedish Mission helped the LELM to overcome their crisis these are the reason four Swedish Missionaries worked in Pandur.

As mentioned earlier, the work and properties of the LELM in Tamil Nadu were transferred in 1916 to the CSM. The Swedish Mission helped the LELM to overcome their crisis this was the reason four Swedish Missionaries worked in Pandur. Even though, Swedish Mission took charge of the work of the LELM but it was not too easy for them to look after the whole field and to establish an administrative body which was recognized by the government.[131]

3.9. Tamil Evangelical Lutheran Church

War interrupted the organic constitutional development with the result, that in 1919 January 14th the Tamil Lutheran congregations that had been tended by Swedish and German Missionaries with

---

127 D. Arthur Jeyakumar, *Bishop Johannes: Sandegren and the British Government of India*, 6.

128 Meyner, *Correspondence between LELM and the Government,* 1914-1919, 3rd November 1915.

129 E. Brutzer, R. Hoffmann, Miss H. Hansen, and Miss E. Von Gernet.

130 J. D. Asirvadam, *Johannes Sandegren: the Third Bishop of Tranquebar* (Chennai: CLS, 1962), 16.

131 W. Hellinger, "*The Leipzig Evangelical Lutheran Mission*" in C. H. Swavely (ed) *The Lutheran Enterprise in India*, 26.

the assistance of Indian pastors formed the Tamil Evangelical Lutheran Churches as an independent body.[132] This Church got her constitution in 1921 and in addition a Bishop as her head.[133] Today, its ministry is mainly concentrated in the state of Tamil Nadu and in certain parts of Karnataka, Andhra Pradesh, Kerala, Pondicherry and Andaman & Nicobar Islands. TELC has 1,05,773 members in around 110 pastorates.[134]

132 http://www.lutheranforum.org/extras/the-lutheran-churches-of-india/ accessed on 12.4.2015.

133 W. Hellinger, "*The Leipzig Evangelical Lutheran Mission*" in C.H. Swavely, *The Lutheran Enterprise in India,* 21.

134 Lutheran Missions.org/history-of-lutherans-in-india-1909-2009 accessed on 12.4.2015.

Chapter 4

Evaluating the Motives and Methods of Leipzig Mission through the voices of Pandur Dalit Christians

Introduction

In this chapter we will discuss the motives of the Leipzig Missionaries and what made them launch the kind of social work they did? Was religious conversion the only motive to do that kind of welfare for the people? This is a common question in many. Let us evaluate the motive of the mission methods used by the missionaries in order to liberate the Dalit people who lived in and around Pandur. What do Dalit Christians of Pandur think about Leipzig missionaries and their work? What are the challenges LELM faced in their field and what is the present project they are involved in Pandur.

4.1. Inducement

In the 1900s, the big question among the Mission societies was: Can legal and financial help be given to Pariahs? There were lots of criticisms about mission societies. The common observation was that the missionaries were converting pariahs offering social welfare.

To answer the above question Rev. Johannes Kabis wrote an article in the magazine, The Harvest Fields Periodical captioned 'Should legal and financial help be given to pariahs?' In his writing he strongly recommended that no society should extend monetary help to poor pariahs with the intention of inducing them to embrace Christianity. He records his disapproval towards the Jesuit missions who were adopting this practice to convert the pariahs. He insisted that, conversely, protestant missionaries would never intentionally provide inducements, underscoring their innocence in the production of impure motives.[135]

But, during the time of famine and in many other difficult situations the protestant missionaries supported the Dalits. But this act was misunderstood by others as inducement. When charity was considered as an inducement it was disappointing and discouraging for the missionaries. But what connection has this question with the mission's work? Is it the duty of a missionary to improve the social, economic, and educational level of the Dalits, or should they rather confine themselves to spiritual work only by preaching the gospel and teaching the Gentiles to observe all things Christ commanded? If we see by the principle of Kabis it is right to see pariahs as an exceptional case. He challenges if anyone is willing to work among pariahs only by preaching and teaching soon he/she will regret what he/she thought. Why Kabis says so is because the life condition of Dalits was so miserable that they needed teachers. But that in itself was not enough, for they needed a pleader and an almoner. We saw in the first chapter how the Dalits were discriminated in various ways and it gives a clear picture of Kabis' statement.[136]

4.1.1. Imperialism

There is a common notion about Christian mission and missionaries. They travel to different countries and try to implement their culture and religion by giving some inducement and by force. Even this

135 Johannes Kabis, *Harvest Field: Should Legal and Financial Help be given to Pariah*? (Mysore: Wesleyan Mission Press, 1897), 362.

136 Johannes Kabis, *Harvest Field: Should Legal and Financial Help be given to Pariah?*, 362.

was the understanding of some of the missionaries' descendants who were living in Germany.

> Rev. Konrad Schomerus and his friends also thought the same way until they arrived in Pandur. When they landed and moved with the Dalit Christians of Pandur they changed their understanding because Dalit Christians of Pandur explained to them how they were oppressed by the upper caste people and how the Leipzig missionaries liberated them from all sorts of oppressions.[137]

Leipzig mission never forced anyone to become Christians (see: 3.6.2) and this is evident in the missionaries' approving the local culture in the Indian Christian marriage system.

4.1.2. Driving Force

Poverty was not the only driving the force for the Dalits to look out for someone to help them, but their disability in the face of various forms of oppressions by the caste people, by the village officials, and even by those higher government servants who were supposed to do justice without consideration of caste and creed. They were deceived by the upper caste people in many ways, i.e., Dalits were compelled by upper caste people to pay a due which they did not have not to pay, or to pay a due the second time as no receipt was given for the first payment, or to pay a loan which they never borrowed on the strength of a forged document. They were uneducated and they were in helpless such situations. Even if they went to the Court, the judgment was not in favor of the Dalits (see: 3.5.8). The only hope for them was the missionaries to whom they had free access and the missionaries were the only ones who had mercy and sympathy for them and were willing to give voice for the voiceless;[138] in short not poverty, but rather mistreatment and injustice which drove Pariahs to the Missionaries.

---

137 Konrad Schomerus Interviewed on 24. January 2015 in Herrmansburg.

138 Johannes Kabis, *Harvest Field: Should Legal and Financial Help be given to Pariah*? 366.

4.1.3. Sacred and Secular

Kabis explained how pariahs' condition was an exceptional one that demanded intervention. Kabis was aware that this still did not fully justify the missionary intervention, for even a Government or the social organization would do just as well. He clearly defines in his article Christianity was not a new form of law or socio-politics. But he strongly believed that bodily and spiritual miseries were so closely interconnected that they could scarcely be separated. "Since a Dalit feels his external distress much more than his spiritual and if we wish to help him only in his spiritual need there may be the risk of him turning away from us as merciless hypocrites."[139]

The problems and challenges faced by Johannes Kabis helped him to write a beautiful article because the Dalits who lived in and around Pandur also faced similar problems in their day to day life. Leipzig missionaries saw it and they were moved with love and compassion to help the Dalits. My next section will explain how really the Leipzig missionaries and their methods liberated the Dalit Christians of Pandur from all sorts of oppressions.

4.2. Education and accommodation

The Dalit theologian Felix Wilfred rightly said that powerlessness of Dalits is due to the absence of education[140] as seen in chapter two (Ref. 2.5.1). The upper caste people did not like or allow a Dalit to be educated. But a school established by the Missionary helped them to get educated and to attain a good level in society. The following voices from Pandur explain how the school established by the missionaries helped them to attain a good level in the society.

> Mr. Pannerselvam said, "People who lived in and around Pandur came to Pandur and got education in the school and attained good status in their life." Once a retired police officer came to him and said, "I was educated in this school and became a police officer. This school helped me to attain

139 Johannes Kabis, *Harvest Field: Should Legal and Financial Help be given to Pariah*? 368.

140 Felix Wilfred, *Dalit Empowerment* (Delhi: ISPCK, 2007), 81.

> a good status in the society.[141] Even Mr. Pannerselvam's father was uneducated but he could study up to 6th standard in the school started by the missionary." His daughters were also educated in the same school. His first daughter is now a nurse and the second daughter a teacher. He said with joy, "Without the Missionaries my daughters would not have got educated."

> According to Mr. Basker, "Through education the missionaries liberated people from oppression; otherwise still the Pandur people would be in oppression doing menial jobs in houses and farms of the high caste people."[142] The schools which were founded and run by the missionaries presented the only opportunity to escape the shackles of their caste.[143]

The Leipzig Missionaries realized that only opening schools would not help the people who were living in around Pandur. They started hostels where food and accommodation were provided to the children especially the Dalit children. The following retired teachers explain how the hostels helped them to get education and attain a good level in the society.

The hostel was started for the poor Dalit children who could not afford education. Food and accommodation were provided free of cost. The only task for the children was to study. The children were educated till 8th standard. In those days, if a person passed 8th standard they could go for higher studies such as teacher training, nursing course, etc.[144]

> Mr. Paulraj a retired teacher said, "If the missionaries had not given us education we should have perished. My father didn't study. They where shepherds and daily wagers. But

141 Mr. Pannerselvam Interviewed on 20 November 2014 in Pandur

142 Mr. Basker Interviewed on 18 November 2014 in kanakaranee.

143 http://www.amycarmichel.bplaced.net/Rudolf_Schomerus.pdf accessed on 3.4.15.

144 Mr. Selvaraj Interviewed on 20 November 2014 in Pandur.

> I became a teacher and it happened because of the Boys' Hostel and schools started by missionaries.[145]

Historian Hugald Grafe rightly said, "The education of *Adi-dravidars* received a momentous stimulus above all; they were filled with a new sense of self-esteem. In 1908, the Madras Depressed Classes conference met at Chidambaram for the first time. Catechist Israel of Pandur (LELM) was its secretary."[146] This shows how Education in Pandur created a big change among the Dalit people who lived in and around Pandur.

4.2.1. Exposure

The Dalits who lived in and around Pandur got different exposure after the arrival of missionaries. After their school education they were sent for higher education to different parts in Tamil Nadu. It helped them to meet new people, with different experiences and social backgrounds. They also got new ideas and plans.

> Mr. Selvaraj says "today the life condition of Pandur Dalit Christians is better than high caste people because of the education and exposure they got from the missionaries. After their school education missionaries sent them to different parts of Tamil Nadu for higher education. The good exposure and the knowledge gained made the Dalits wiser than the upper caste people."[147]

4.2.2. Breaking the barriers

The Dalits were considered 'untouchables' but the schools established by the missionaries in Pandur broke this kind of understanding because the school not only gave education but also helped to bring all caste people to one place. The upper caste people did not have any other option for education except Kabis' School. So, the upper caste and lower caste had to study in the same school and the school made a great impact on the society.

---

145 Mr. Paulraj Interviewed on 18 November 2014 in Pandur.

146 Hugald Grafe, *History of Christianity in Tamil Nadu from 1800 to 1975*, 216.

147 Mr. Selvaraj Interviewed 20.November 2014 in Pandur.

> Mr. Selvaraj says, "In our surrounding there were no schools and so all caste people came to the schools established by the missionaries in Pattarai Perumbudur and got education."[148]

Not only such schools but even the sewing school brought everyone to the same place N.R. Elizabeth who is in charge for the tailoring school said:

> "This tailoring school was not only for the Christians but also for all people regardless of religion. Even Muslim and Hindu people are trained here and many became tailoring teachers in different institutions."[149]

4.2.3. Healing

This word means a lot to the Pandur Dalits because the Dalits were healed by the missionaries in all areas of their life, i.e., the Dalits in Pandur were psychologically wounded by the upper caste people as untouchables and people of low self-esteem. But when the missionaries showed them that they were loved by God and were more valuable in the sight of God it gave them inner healing and helped in their psychological well-being.

Physically they were infected and affected by various kinds of diseases (see.3.5.6). Missionaries tried their best to cure people from their diseases. Many people were benefitted by the medical work done by the missionaries and especially the pregnant women. Pandur clinic helped women to deliver their babies safely. Following voices of Pandur Dalit Christians explain how the medical facilities were in Pandur before the arrival of missionaries and how they were later benefitted by their medical work.

> Mr. Samraj says, there were no medical facilities before the missionaries came here. People had to go to Thiruvallur. But even in Thiruvallur the medical facilities were not so good.[150]

148 Mr. Selvaraj Interviewed on 20 November 2014 in Pattrai Perrambathur.

149 N.R Elizabeth Interviewed on 19 November 2014 in Pandur.

150 Mr. Samraj Interviewed on 18 November 2014 in Kanakaranee.

> Mr. Basker said that once he met with a fire accident. His eyes were burnt. The Leipzig Missionary Lydia Runke helped him and gave him medicine. Mr. Basker said with tears "but for the missionary I would be dead by now."[151]

The above mentioned two statements give us a clear picture of how the medical facilities were lacking before the arrival missionaries and how the people from Pandur benefited after the missionaries arrived.

4.2.4. Income

The economic condition of the Dalits who lived in and around Pandur was very bad. (see. 2.12.3). Missionaries tried their best to improve their lot. In order to uplift the economic condition of the people the first and foremost thing they thought beneficial was acquisition of land. Kabis strongly believed if Dalits wanted to be socially and economically secure they should have land to do agriculture. For that he approached the government to give the waste land to the Dalits and the Leipzig mission and his friends from Germany supported him to purchase lands. He succeeded in his efforts. Labourers became land owners. Dalits started to cultivate their land and produced their own crop and earned money.

> Mr. Selvaraj the church committee member in Pattarai Paramabathur says, "The Dalits did not own lands in their earlier days. But the missionaries bought land and gave them for agriculture in order to uplift their economic condition."[152]

Missionaries knew water was the prominent need for agriculture but in India monsoon was not regular. The missionaries realised this and they dug many wells in and around Pandur. These wells helped the Christians to do agriculture without any hurdles and to get income. The following statement by my Basker gives how these wells were useful for them.

---

151 Mr. Basker Interviewed on 18 November 2014 in Kanakaranee.

152 Mr. Selvaraj Interviewed on 17 November 2014 in Pattrai Perrambathur.

> Mr. Selvaraj says, "The Missionaries dug the well in and around Pandur and installed motors to draw water from the well. He says these wells are very useful to do agriculture."[153]

Even though, they had very good wells failing monsoons too often caused crop failure. The agricultural produce also fetched low prices and this was a serious handicap to fulfill their expected economic development. Though, the enterprise was not very encouraging the congregation maintained their stability in good times and in bad times.[154]

Not only through land or agriculture but also through education the economic condition of the Dalits started improving. Dalits started to work as teachers, nurses in government schools. Working in a Government school as a teacher was a great privilege in India. A government school teacher while receiving a good salary also enjoyed all the benefits of the welfare schemes of the government.

Before Missionaries came to India education was a privilege available only to the high caste and therefore, they only stood the chance for government jobs. The unprivileged Dalits were illiterates and therefore they could not dream of Government jobs. "Leipzig missionaries gave us education and through that we got good jobs and it helped us to attain a good economic condition in our Life."[155]

Tailoring school which was started by the missionaries helped the women who were living in and around Pandur earn money for their day to day life.

Manjula is a tailoring teacher in Pandur Tailoring School. Her husband died. She has two sons. She said that as a properly trained tailor she gets good business. "It's very much helpful to me" she says.[156]

---

153 Mr. Selvaraj Interviewed on 20 November 2014 in Pandur.

154 W. Hellinger "*The Leipzig Evangelical Lutheran Mission*" in C.H. Swavely (ed) *Lutheran Enterprises in India,* 1706-1952, 21.

155 Arul Mary Interviewed on 20.December 2014 in Pandur.

156 Mrs. Manjula Interviewed on 25.November 2014 in Pandur.

4.2.5. Female empowerment

Social empowerment is understood as the process of developing a sense of autonomy and self-confidence, and acting individually and collectively to change social relationships. The institutions and discourses that exclude poor people keep them in poverty. Self-decision regarding education, participation, mobility, economic independency, public speaking, awareness and exercise of rights, political participation and many more factors ensure women empowerment. In short women empowerment is the breaking of personal limitation.

Another model is empowerment of women through the education of girls by founding schools for them. Indian Dalit scholars say Dalit women are doubly oppressed in Indian society because first they are Dalits and secondly they are women. "addupu oothum pengaluku kalvi eaaduku" and that means women are meant only for cooking and so why do they need education? This kind of misunderstanding was prevailing in those days in india specially in Pandur.

The missionaries rightly found out that lack of education was the reason why Dalit women were not able to come out of their miserable condition. Among converted Dalits there was a better consciousness of education. They somehow sent their children to school, thinking that at least they will have better lives in future.[157]

But, after the missionaries came to Pandur and realised that education could empower the Dalit women they started a school both for boys and girls and thus Dalit women started to get education. They also realized that only a school was not enough. Indian culture would not allow women to go alone anywhere. If they went out they must return home before it became dark. It was not easy for Dalit girls who lived in and around Pandur to go to school because there was no transport. So, the missionaries started girls' hostels where they could stay and get education. It was a great help for the Dalit girls to get education and be in a safe place.

157 V. Devasahayam, *Frontiers of Dalit Theology* (Madras: Gurukul Lutheran Theological College & Research Institute, Madras, 1997), 108.

> Mrs. Indrani said, "In the earlier days the Girl children who lived in and around Pandur could not get education and so the missionaries built hostels where boys and girls could come and stay and get education. Mrs. Indrani was educated in the Kabis School. She studied there 1-8th and thereafter she was sent for a teacher training course and she became a teacher."[158]

4.2.6. Undignified to Dignified

Self dignity was the big question for the Dalits. Even their dresses were considered untouchable (see.2.12.1). After conversion the Dalits gained their dignity. The missionaries helped the Dalit Christians get their self dignity.

> "Mr. Devadoss who worked in TELC church as a sexton for 50 years says that the Dalits were treated in undignified ways. He says the upper caste people called the Dalits not by their name but by their caste name (*dai parahapiya* ---the most hurting and abusive derogatory term).
>
> They employed the Dalits in their fields and outside their houses but they never allowed them inside their houses. The Dalits must sit only in cow sheds, the unclean and dingy places, and they were given only stale food. It is the missionaries who changed the scenario in Pandur."[159]

Dalit Christians buried their dead ones in the cemetery. (See: 3.5.10) Hindu high caste people brought their dead to the Dalit colony and burnt them because according to them Dalits were untouchable. The dead bodies were also untouchable. But Missionary Heller approached the Hindu people who were burning their dead bodies and protested that they should not use the Dalit colony to bury their dead. The practice was stopped immediately. Now, if we have a cemetery to bury our departed in a dignified way it's only because of the missionaries.[160]

158 Mrs. Indrani Interviewed on 18 November 2014 in Kanakaranee.

159 Mr. Devadoss Interviewed on 18 November 2014 in Pandur.

160 Mr. Basker Interviewed on 18 November 2014 in Pandur.

4.2.7. Forerunners for counter culture

The Missionaries challenged Brahminic culture because the Brahminic culture and ideology were based on purity-pollution, high and low, sacred-profane binary. The Missionaries challenged such attitudes by their actions; for example the Brahmins never touched the Dalits and the belongings of the Dalits; but the missionaries touched the untouchable and enjoyed the Dalit cultural instrument called *Parai* (drum). According to Brahminic culture *Parai* (drum) is a polluted instrument and it should be played only for a funeral; for the instrument was made by means of a dead cow skin. But missionaries challenged this kind of Brahminic superstition.

Rev. Alwin beautifully explained how the *parai* (drum) was used by the Dalits during the time of carol services and it was appreciated by the German Missionaries.[161]

4.2.8. Purpose of Religion

The caste system remains more or less intact because of the solid support it derives from the other religions. Devasahayam clearly says that without Hinduism it is impossible for caste system to survive. The Brahmins died to their association with the religion and temple, captured the apex of the feudal pyramid and excluded Dalits from the temple by the notion of ritual purity and pollution.[162]

On the other hand the religion introduced by the missionaries is totally different from Hinduism. Brahmins used religion to prevent Dalits entering the temple but missionaries used religion to invite people inside the temple. Brahmins used religion to prohibit education to Dalits but missionaries used religion to educate people. Brahmins used religion to create low self-esteem among Dalits but missionaries used religion to build self-confidence in Dalits. In short the Brahmins used Hinduism for oppressive purposes but missionaries used Christianity for a liberation purpose.

161 Alwin Gehring, *Johannes Kabis: A Father of Pariah,* 68.

162 V. Devasahayam, *Outside the Camp: Bible Studies in Dalit Perspective* (Madras: Gurukul Lutheran Theological College & Research Institute, 1992), 10.

> "I am surprised when I heard that a particular group of people (Dalits) was oppressed by the upper caste people in name of religion (*Hinduism*). Interestingly both are from the same religion. But new the religion (Christianity) showed them a different view of religion, i.e., not oppressive but liberative. If conversion is done by force I won't accept it but in Pandur people embraced Christianity willingly" said by the "Great Granddaughter of Missionary Johannes Kabis."[163]

4.3. Living with the people

4.3.1. Identified with the Dalits

When the Leipzig Missionaries came to Pandur and its surrounding area, the Paraiyars lived as virtual slaves in bonded labor and poverty. They were despised as untouchables and kept outside the caste system. Even their shadow was considered polluting. They were not allowed to learn. In the best of times they were undernourished, poorly clothed and lived in miserable houses. In the worst of times starvation, sickness and death were common. Missionary Kabis and his wife arrived at Pandur and started to do Evangelism and social work. Amidst difficulties Kabis and the Leipzig missionaries could bring about a great transformation in their region. During the time of famine and other kinds of trials Leipzig Missionaries identified themselves with the Dalits in and around Pandur. It was not easy for them to accommodate with the Indian climate and environment but they did their best. Missionary Schomerus lost his one year old son and later Schomerus himself died of typhoid at Pandur. But until his death he worked for the welfare of the Dalits in and around Pandur.

4.3.2. House Visiting

The Missionaries and their wives played an important role in visiting people in their own houses to teach the scripture and for encouraging people to pursue secular studies. Missionaries were not only visiting people for education and evangelical work but also for medical work. Schomerus wife also often visited the sick and elderly people in and

163 Mrs. Adelheid Wedel, Interviewed on 11 September 2014 in Berlin.

around Pandur and provided them medicines which were sent to her by friends from Germany.[164]

Early missionaries were interested in preaching and spreading the gospel across cultures and social customs. However, some people were not allowed to come inside the village- like people who are infected by Leprosy. But the Leipzig missionaries visited such people in their houses and gave them regular treatments in their clinics.

There was a leper among the Christians in Pandur. The man could not live in the village so he built a small hut one kilometre away from the village and lived alone. His relatives brought him food every day and he was dependent on them fully. But one day, Schomerus Rudolf and Wilhelm Ruckdaeschel saw him crawling in front of the hut. Rudolf Schomerus conducted a small worship service for the man singing a song and reading a text. Rudolf Schomerus gave a little speech and closed the celebration with a prayer. The man was happy over this divine service. He did this in the days when people in India strongly believed that even if a person spoke or went inside the house of a leper he/she was infected already. But this bold approach of the Missionary showed and opened the eyes of the people that leprosy was not a contagious disease.[165]

4.3.3. Bible women

Missionaries conducted bible studies for the bible women and sent them for the village ministry. These bible women went to every village in and around Pandur and taught them the bible. They also supplied information to the missionaries about the needs of the people as well the needs of the village churches. The bible women were even involved in medical work at the clinics started in Pandur.[166] Still this wing of the ministry is very active in Pandur and at present, there are two bible women in Pandur pastorate - Mrs. Arul Mary and Mrs. Dahana Mani.

---

164 http://www.amycarmichel.bplaced.net/Rudolf_Schomerus.pdf accessed on 3.4.15.

165 J.W. Ruckdaeschel, *1911-1916 Missionar der Evangelical Lutheran Leipziger HeidenMission auf der Station Pandur bei Madras in Südindien,* unpublished material, 51-52.

166 Catharine Vimala, *Pandur in Tranquebar Mission History*, 47.

> "Mr. Selvaraj said missionary Froelich was so interested in house visiting that she always took the bible women with her and visited the home of each and every congregation member in order to know them personally and about their problems and difficulties."[167]

4.3.4. Accepting the local Culture

We cannot say missionaries accepted every aspect of local culture of the Tamil people, but they accepted some very important cultural practices; for example during the time of marriage, according to the Tamil culture, the bride groom ties *Tali* around a bride's neck. *Tali* are piece of jewelry usually made of gold and it hangs on a yellow thread and it is proof that the woman is married. Once Missionary Wilhelm had to wait for a long time to solemnize a marriage because the *Tali* did not arrive; only after the *Tali* arrived he solemnized the wedding.[168]

4.4. Living Christian values

4.4.1. Caring and sharing

In the early days missionaries had a serious situation of having to take care of the new converts and their children from the persecution of the non-converts and from terrible famines. Owing to famine and bad harvest there were times when it was very difficult to support the poor Christians. Sometimes the missionaries parted with their last penny. Kabis' friends sent some gift to support the poor Christians and so he took care of the Pandur Christians in times of their need. The missionaries shared their money and their resources with the people in their mission-fields. Historian Hugald Grafe says Johannes Kabis spent from his own pocket to purchase lands and for going to the law -courts to help the Adidravidars who approached him for help in getting justice.[169]

---

167 Mr. Selvaraj, Interviewed on 20 November 2014 in Pandur.

168 J.W. Ruckdaeschel, *1911-1916 Missionar der Evangelical Lutheran Leipziger Heiden Mission auf der Station Pandur bei Madras in Südindien,* unpublished material, 49-50.

169 Hugald Grafe, *History of Christianity in Tamil Nadu from 1800 to1975,* 216.

> "Mr. Selvaraj said that during the time of famine the Missionary Heller went to the people in and around Pandur and gave them milk and dresses."[170]

4.4.2. Prayerful and Faithful Life

Prayer is the important role in the of missionaries' life. The pioneer Missionary of Leipzig missionary Johannes Kabis regularly visited the sick people and prayed for them. He never hesitated even when some people called him late in the night for prayer. Once he was invited by Mr. Ponnapen to his house because his daughter was very sick. Her body, hands, feet and face were swollen. Kabis went and knelt with the family and prayed that God might heal the sick daughter and help the family to be steadfast in their faith in the midst of the crisis.

> Mr. Basker said that "once people started to dig a well but they couldn't find water. They digged still deeper and as deeper as possible; but they couldn't get water. Then they went to Schomerus and informed him. Schomerus came to the spot knelt down and prayed. While he was returning to his room a man was running behind him shouting with joy "*ayyha kenathula thaneer vanduch*ee"- it means Sir Water has come in the well. Basker concludes that the missionaries lived faithfully and led a prayerful life and set good examples for us."[171]

4.4.3. Missionary accountability

It was not easy for Leipzig Missionaries to accommodate with the Indian climate and environment but they did their best. Missionary Schomerus lost his one year old son and later Schomerus himself died of typhoid at Pandur. But until his death he worked for the welfare of the Dalits in and around Pandur. Even though, Leipzig missionaries faced lot of problems and crisis they were faithful in their Missionary Work.

170 Mr. Selvaraj, Interviewed on 20 November 2014 in Pandur.

171 Mr. Basker Interviewed on 18 November 2014 in Kanakaranee.

4.5. Challenges

4.5.1. Famine

The high mortality in times of famine (1866; 1876-78; 1895-1900) affected the congregations very much. The famine affected in and around Pandur also. Leipzig missionaries faced big challenges due to famine. Christians came to Kabis asking for some jobs. During that time the Patterei Perumbudur Chapel construction work was in process. So, Kabis could employ 200 Christians every day. But day by day the crowd kept increasing; the money given by the Church Council depleted; now instead of saying 'no' to people, Kabis spent his money to give salary to the workers.[172] For some people Kabis gave job in the agricultural school because that was the time agricultural schools began to emerge. Due to the famine many migrated to Burma. The famine [173] shook the faith of the believers; but Kabis did his best to strengthen the faith of the believers' through his teaching helping them to survive in the midst of the difficult times.

4.5.2. Casteism

There were other difficulties too. The chief among them was the caste-question. The Leipzig Mission had a more tolerant attitude towards caste in the church than had any other mission. Considering caste observance as practiced among the Christians a mere social system without religious significance, the Leipzig Missionaries were willing to make certain concessions to caste in their congregation. They expected that caste-feelings would gradually disappear from the church. In the meantime all other missions contended that caste system had a religious character and rested on the idea of the difference of man's religious value; no compromise, therefore, in regard to caste should be allowed in the Church. The Leipzig Mission kept itself aloof from the consensus of opinion of the whole body of the Evangelical Missionary Societies.[174] In the first

172 Friedhelm Beyreiss, *Johannes Kabis: Ein Leben für die Mission in Südindien*, 119.

173 Alwin Gehring, *Johannes Kabis: A Father of Pariah,* 71.

174 Julius Richter, translated by Sydney H. Moore, *A History of Missions in India*, (New York: H. Revell Company, 1908), 261.

South Indian Missionary Conference, which was held in May 1858 with the participation of about 200 representatives from various Evangelical Missions in South India and Ceylon, a resolution was passed condemning the Leipzig Mission for its lenient attitude to the caste system.[175]

Anglican Mission forced people to denounce Casteism and it created some tension inside the church. Some went back to the Roman church and some to Hinduism. LELM Missionaries strongly believed that caste-spirit should be fought but force and compulsion should not be used and that setting a good example would help eradicates Casteism from the church. Slowly but steadily the caste spirit in the congregations was overcome. It lost its domineering position from where it had mocked at the spirit of love. The LELM Missionaries strongly believed eradicating Casteism was not a one day event but a continuous process. They started to empower the Dalits in all areas of their life to set a good example to the upper caste people to press into their mind- set that all are equal in the sight of God. This approach worked in Pandur very well. The statement below by Mr. Samraj will explain this.

> "In the earlier days Casteism was overwhelming in and around Pandur but things began to change after the missionaries came and empowered the Dalits in all areas of their life. Today everything has changed. The High caste people are coming to our homes and we are going to their homes and are eating meals together."[176] Yes we can see that Casteism has lost its domineering position in and around Pandur today.

4.6. Present LELM Projects in Pandur

In order to promote understanding, relationship and harmony among communities and to provide and maintain an atmosphere conducive to further social developments, LELM devised partnership programs with TELC. There are three important projects: Firstly the Mission

175 Henrietta Bugge, *Mission and Tamil Society,* 1840-1900 (Wiltshire: The Cromwell Press Ltd, 1994), 63.

176 Mr. Samraj Interviewed on 18 Novemeber, 2014 in Kanakaranee.

to the North, secondly sending volunteers to TELC and the third project is a combined project with the Amy Carmichael organization. We can see the details below:

4.6.1. Mission to the North

This program was started in 2006. LELM invited visitors from the partner churches in TELC and one delegate from each partner church. The delegates stay for 3 months in LELM and share their life and faith experience in their own church. It is a very good opportunity for intercultural learning experience for both sides. Selection of delegates is done by the partner church. LELM has given full freedom to the Church Council to send people from India to Germany. This year the church council of TELC sent Mrs. Jebamani Devakirubai from Pandur to Germany.[177]

4.6.2. Volunteers program

LELM has two kinds of Volunteer programs with the partner church. Firstly, LELM Invites two people from their partner church and these volunteers work in old age homes and rehabilitation centers for one year. Secondly, to foster intercultural ties and exchanges, 5 men and women are offered a voluntary service opportunity in TELC churches every year for up to 6 months. Every year one volunteer is sent to Pandur.[178]

4.6.3. Supporting the Dalit children

Amy Carmichael is a private social organization which has partnership with TELC Froelich Home in Pandur and in LELM. This organization has around 110 memberships. These members are the supporters of the children who are in Pandur called Froelich and Heller Home. In this group there are three missionary descendants who also supported the Pandur Dalit children.[179]

177 http://www.lmw-mission.de/de/missiontothenorth.html accessed on 29.4.2015.

178 http://www.lmw-mission.de/de/ueber-das-lmw.html accessed on 29.4.2015.

179 http://www.amycarmichel.bplaced.net/information-german.html accessed on 3.4.2015.

The descendents of the missionaries are happy supporting the children where their grandparents worked and often they visit Pandur.

Chapter 5

Conclusion

Leipzig missionaries bore witness to the Gospel of Christ by words and deeds. Leipzig missionaries did their work according to what their Bible taught. They established mission-stations wherever they had the opportunity to preach the gospel. The mission station established in Pandur brought good news to the Dalits both spiritually and socially. Proclaiming the Gospel was the prime motive for the LELM but they did not stop there. When they saw the pathetic condition of the Dalits in and around Pandur they rendered their helping hands to uplift them. LELM missionaries were careful in their work. They never offered inducement to the Dalits to embrace Christianity. During the famine many people came to Kabis and wanted to become Christians. Their motive was to get some welfare from him. But Kabis firmly refused to accept them. But he offered some help to them also.

If Kabis and his colleagues did the liberation and welfare work they did it out of Love. Since they experienced Christ's love they showed the same love to the Pandur Dalits. Throughout my research what I found was that the Leipzig missionaries did not have any inner agenda or motive for helping the Dalits who lived in and around Pandur. The driving force of the missionaries to help the Pandur Dalits was the love of God. The Dalits were mistreated and injustice was done to them in their everyday life. Dalits were always looked down upon by the fellow citizens. The upper caste people never treated the Dalits as human beings. Their rights were denied by the upper caste people. But their plight was dramatically changed by the love and care shown to them by the Leipzig missionaries. Now the ones who were 'no people' became the people of God.

The missionaries strongly believed that their main task was preaching the Gospel besides developing ways and means to liberate people from social evils. The missionaries felt that they were not only messengers of faith but also of love. They also felt that only preaching God's word without helping them will be like sounding brass or tinkling cymbals. Mere sympathy towards Dalits was not considered as a sufficient solution of their social problems; steps must be taken liberate them from their misery.

In fact the missionaries followed the example of our Lord and savior Jesus Christ in their ministry because our Lord was not only the teacher of love, but whose life also was the first example of a life of Love. Love was embodied in Him. Leipzig missionaries followed the six recognized works of mercy which Jesus Christ showed in the gospels, i.e., feeding the hungry, giving water to the thirsty, clothing the naked, protecting the stranger, tending the sick, visiting the prisoner, and to these the church and missionaries added one more - burying the dead.[180]

The missionaries fed the hungry people by buying and providing parcels of lands for them to do agriculture. At present, TELC is holding all the Lands and members of the Pandur Dalit community are paying a nominal amount as subscription and use the land for their various projects like agriculture, housing and other social development programs. LELM Missionaries provided clothes to the poor through the sewing schools; they dug wells to provide water to the thirsty; when the high caste people around them treated them as strangers the missionaries protected them from all kinds of oppressions. They healed the sick by training nurses and medical workers and by providing hospitals and clinics. The oppressed people were also provided with legal aid whenever the upper caste

180 Johannes Kabis, *Harvest Field: Should Legal and Financial Help be given to Pariah?* 369.

people foisted false cases on them; the missionaries were the voice for the voiceless. The Dalits had no place to bury their dead while the upper class people freely buried their dead in the Dalit colony as they considered both the Dalits and the dead bodies as untouchables. Today if Pandur people have a cemetery for their dead it is because of the missionaries.

The missionaries did all these developmental works in the absence of modern roads and transports. They walked miles together every day and personally attended to the needs of the people and rendered service in its real sense. Gradually, the age old social order gave way to a new social order and hence, a new, cultured, civilized and educated society related to the development of Tamil people began to emerge. The once undignified people were transformed into dignified people; the uneducated became the educated community; the landless laborers became land owners.

According to Pandur Dalit Christians the Leipzig missionaries were their friends in their need and the champions in their oppressed situations. This is the conclusion I arrived at after my visit and personal interactions with the Pandur Dalit Christians.

Bibliography

Books

Asirvadam, J. D. *Johannes Sandegren: The Third Bishop of Tranquebar.* Chennai: CLS, 1962.

Badley, B. H. *Indian Missionary Directory and Memorial Volume.* Lucknow: American Methodist Mission, 1876.

Barbara, R. Joshi, ed., *"Untouchable, Voice of the Dalit Liberation Movement: Dalit Panthers Manifesto.* Delhi: Select Book Service Syndicate, 1986.

Becker, Carl. *History of the Catholic Missions in North East India,* 1890-1915. Shillong: Firma KLM, 1980.

Beyreiss, Friedhelm. *Johannes Kabis: Ein Leben für die Mission in Südindien.* Jever: Sós Éva, Jászszentandrás, 2001. Translated by Lena.

Clarke, Sathianathan. *Dalit Theology in the Twenty-first Century Discordant Voices, Discerning Pathways.* Oxford Press: New Delhi, 2010.

Devasahayam, V. *Frontiers of Dalit Theology.* Madras: Gurukul Lutheran Theological College & Research Institute, Madras, 1997.

Devasahayam, V. *Outside the Camp: Bible Studies in Dalit Perspective.* Madras: Gurukul Lutheran Theological College & Research Institute, 1992.

Devasahayam, V. *Pollution, Poverty and Powerlessness,* in Arvind P. Nirmal (ed) *A Reader in Dalit Theology,* Chennai: Gurukul Lutheran Theological College & Research Institute, 2007.

Estborn, Sigfrid, "The Tranquebar Mission", in C. H. Swavely (ed) *Lutheran Enterprises in India,* 1706-1952, Madras: Federation of Evangelical Lutheran Churches in India, 1952.

Gehring, Alwin. *Johannes Kabis Ein Vater der Paria.* Leipzig: Erlagen der Evanglich Lutherlichen Mission, n.d.

Grafe, Hugald. *History of Christianity in Tamilnadu from 1800 to 1975*. Bangalore: Church History Association of India, 1990.

Grafe, Hugald. *Kirche unter Dalits, Adivasi und Kastenleuten in Südindien*. Berlin: LIT, Publication, 2013.

Handmann, R. *Die Ev. Luth. Tamulen Mission*. Leipzig, 1903.

Hellinger, W. "The Leipzig Evangelical Lutheran Mission" in C. H. Swavely (ed) *Lutheran Enterprises in India,* 1706-1952.

Henrietta Bugge, *Mission and Tamil Society,* 1840-1900. Wiltshire: The Cromwell Press Ltd, 1994.

Hudson, Dennis D. *Protestant Origins in India: Tamil Evangelical Christians, 1707-1835*, Richmond, Surrey: William B. Eerdmans Publishing & Co, 2000.

Iyyer, Samuel. *History of Tranquebar Mission*. Madras: The Tranquebar Printing & Publishing House, 1955.

John, C. B. Webster, *From Indian Church to Indian Theology: An attempt at Theological Construction,* in Arvind P. Nirmal (ed), *A Reader in Dalit Theology.* Chennai: Gurukul Lutheran Theological College & Research Institute, 2007.

Manickam, S. *The Social Setting of Christian Conversion in South India: The Impact of the Wesleyan Methodist Missionaries on the Trichy-Tanjore-Diocese with Special Reference to the Harijan Communities of the Mass Movement Area,* 1820-1937. Wiesbaden: Franz Steiner Verlag 1977.

Massey, James. *Roots: A Concise History of Dalits.* Delhi: The Indian Society for Promoting Christian Knowledge, 1994, {1991}.

Prabhakar, M. E. "The Search for a Dalit Theology," in Prabhakar, (ed) *Toward a Dalit Theology.* Delhi: The Indian Society for Promoting Christians Knowledge, 1988.

Rev. Meyner, *Correspondence between LELM and the Government,* 1914-1919, *3rd November 1915.*

Richter, Julius. Translated by Sydney, Moore H. *A History of Missions in India*. New York: H. Revell Company, 1908.

Ruckdaeschel, J.W. *1911-1916 Missionar der Evangelical Lutheran Leipziger HeidenMission auf der Station Pandur bei Madras in Südindien.* Translated J. R. Jayabalan Robert, unpublished material.

Vimala, Catharine. *Pandur in Tranquebar Mission History*. Chennai: Bethel, 2009.

Wolf, L. B. (ed) *Missionary Heroes of the Lutheran Church.* Philadelphia: The Lutheran Publication Society, 1911.

Wilfred, Felix. *Dalit Empowerment.* Delhi: ISPCK, 2007.

Zelliot, Eleanor, *Untouchable to Dalit.* New Delhi: Manohar Publication, 1992.

Journals

Antony Raj, "The Dalit Christian Reality in Tamilnadu," Jeevadhara 22 (1992) 95-112, 96.

Jeyakumar, Arthur D. *Bishop Johannes Sandegren and the British Government of India*, Indian Church History Review, Mumbai: Indian Church History Review, Vol. XXX, Number 1, June 1996.

Kabis, Johannes. *Harvest Field: Should Legal and Financial Help be given to Pariah?.* (Mysore: Wesleyan Mission Press, 1897), 362.

Kabis, Johannes. *Palmzweige aus ostindischen Missionsfelde* (Leipzig: Verlag der Evanglical Lutheran Mission, 1898), 12. Transalted by Rev. Irene Heinke.

Massey, James. *Christian Dalits: A Historical Perspective, Journal of Dharma* 16 (1991), 44-60.

Webliography

http://www.lmw-Mission.de/de/Missionar-13.html (accessed 27 March 2015)

http://www.lmw-Mission.de/de/Missionar-126.html (accessed 27 March 2015)

http://www.lmw-Mission.de/de/Missionar-187.html (accessed 27 March 2015) http://www.lmw-Mission.de/de/Missionar-226.html (accessed 30 March 2015)

http://www.lmw-Mission.de/de/Missionar-237.html (accessed 30 March 2015)

http://www.lmw-Mission.de/de/Missionar-253.html (accessed 30 March 2015)

http://www.lutheranforum.org/extras/the-lutheran-churches-of-india/ (accessed 12 April 2015)

http://www.LutheranMissions.org/history-of-lutherans-in-india-1909-2009 (accessed 12 April 2015)

http://www.amycarmichel.bplaced.net/Rudolf_Schomerus.pdf (accessed 3 April 2015)

http://www.indianetzone.com/47/history_tiruvallur_district.html (accessed 17 February 2015)

http://saspublisher.com/wp-content/uploads/2014/04/SAJB-24295-306.pdf (accessed 24 February 2015)

http://www.indianetzone.com/47/history_tiruvallur_district.htm (accessed17 February 2015)

http://www.onefivenine.com/india/villages/Thiruvallur/Poondi/Pandur (accessed 2 March 2015)

http://news.nationalgeographic.com/news/2003/06/0602_030602_untouchables.html (accessed 24 February 2015)

http://www.census2011.co.in/data/village/629037-Pandur-tamil-nadu.html (accessed 24 February 2015)

http://www.census2011.co.in/city.php (accessed 24 February 2015)

http://navsarjan.org/navsarjan/Dalits/whoareDalits (accessed 24 May 2015)

http://idsn.org/countries/india/ (accessed 24 May 2015)

http://www.thomasschirrmacher.net/blog/when-indian-Dalits-convert-to-christianity-or-islam- they-lose-social-welfare-benefits-and-rights-they-are-guaranteed-under-the-constitution/ (accessed on 24 May 2015)

http://www.rediff.com/news/2005/feb/11Dalit.html (accessed 24 May 2015)

Appendix A

List of Interviewees

Mrs. Adelheid Wedel, Interviewed on 11 September 2014 in Berlin.

Mrs. Arul Mary Interviewed on 20 December 2014 in Pandur.

Mr. Basker Interviewed on 18 November 2014 in Kanakaranee.

Mr. Devadoss Interviewed on 18 November 2014 in Pandur.

Mrs. Indrani Interviewed on 18 November 2014 in Kanakaranee.

Rev. Konrad Schomoerus Interviewed on 24 January 2015 in Herrmansburg.

Mrs. Manjula Interviewed on 25 November 2014 in Pandur.

Mrs. N.R. Elizabeth Interviewed on 19 November 2014 in Pandur.

Mr. Pannerselvam Interviewed on 20 November 2014 in Pandur.

Mr. Paulraj Interviewed on 18 November 2014 in Pandur.

Mr. Samraj Interviewed 18 November 2014 in Kanakaranee.

Mr. Samikanu Interviewed on 17 November 2014 in Pattrai Perrambathur.

Mr. Selvaraj Interviewed on 20 November 2014 in Pandur.

Mr. Selvaraj Interviewed on 20 November 2014 in Pattrai Perrambathur.

Appendix B

Questionnaire

Dear Sir/Madam,

This questionnaire relates to my research in Theological studies, on "**Dalit Christians of Pandur: Remembering how Leipzig Missionaries liberated them from Oppression.**"

1. What was your ancestor's religion?
2. Which caste your ancestors belong?
3. What was the occupation of your ancestors?
4. What was the education qualification for your ancestors?
5. What was the situation of Dalits in Pandur in earlier days?
6. What was the social, economical and educational condition of Dalits in earlier days?
7. What was the Life condition of Pandur women in earlier days?
8. What was the life condition of Dalit women in earlier days?
9. What was the cultural & political situation in Pandur like in their days?
10. How did your forefather became Christian and what changed in their lives?
11. How did you become Christian?

12. Who preached the Gospel to your ancestor's?
13. Who was the first missionary who came to Pandur and what have you heard about him?
14. How you see mission work Leipzig mission in Pandur?
15. How did Leipzig mission contributed to the empowerment of the Dalits in Pandur?
16. What way Leipzig Mission Helped you come up in your Life situation?
17. Who started the Kabis higher secondary school?
18. Who started the Girls and Boys hostel?
19. Who started the Tailoring school for women?
20. Who started clinic in Pandur?
21. How you see the mission work of Leipzig missionaries?

Appendix C

Maps and Photos

1. Pandur and its surrounding[181]

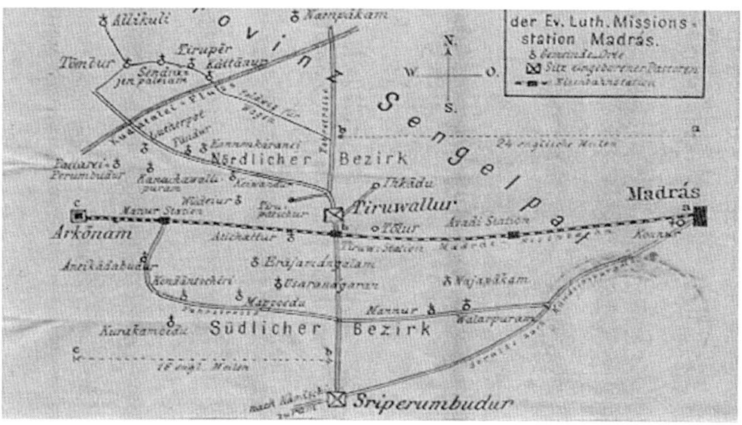

181 Friedhelm Beyreiss, *Johannes Kabis: Ein Leben für die Mission in Südindien,* (Jever: Sós Éva, Jászszentandrás, 2001), 88.

2. Pandur kadhirallayam, 1909[182]

3. Harvest Festivals in Pandur (N.D)[183]

182 Alwin Gehring, *Johannes Kabis: A Father of Pariah,* 73.

183 Alwin Gehring, *Johannes Kabis: A Father of Pariah,* 67.

4. Sewing School in Pandur (N.D)[184,185]

184 Alwin Gehring, *Johannes Kabis: A Father of Pariah*, 47.

185 In this photo Kabis' wife is teaching sewing to the Dalit girls. Kabis is sitting in a chair but his wife is sitting among the students. According to the Indian culture man will not sit next to a woman or among women. Even today this tradition is very strictly observed in the Indian churches. It shows Kabis accepted some very important culture practices.